ADVANCED TOPICS IN MULTIMEDIA RESEARCH

Edited by **Sagarmay Deb**

Advanced Topics in Multimedia Research
Edited by Sagarmay Deb

Published by InTech
Janeza Trdine 9, 51000 Rijeka, Croatia

Publishing Process Manager Daria Nahtigal

Technical Editor Teodora Smiljanic

Cover Designer InTech Design Team

Additional hard copies can be obtained from orders@intechopen.com

Advanced Topics in Multimedia Research, Edited by Sagarmay Deb
p. cm.
ISBN 978-953-51-0078-2

For EU product safety concerns:
IN TECH d.o.o., Prolaz Marije Krucifikse Kozulić 3, 51000 Rijeka, Croatia,
info@intechopen.com or visit our website at intechopen.com.

Meet the editor

Sagarmay Deb is an international consultant and researcher in the field of Information Technology. He received his MS in Statistics from Gauhati University, India, MBA from Long Island University, USA, and PhD from The University of Southern Queensland, Australia. His research interests are multimedia databases, content-based image retrieval, various indexing techniques and electronic commerce. He contributes to books on multimedia databases, attends international conferences and writes research papers for international journals. He has edited two research publications and written one book on multimedia. He currently works at the University of Central Queensland, Australia, and is involved in teaching and research works. Marquis Who's Who, a well-known publisher of biographies of people of notable achievements, has included his biography in their 7th Edition of Who's Who in Science and Engineering. In addition, his biography has been included in the 21st century issue of the 2000 Outstanding Scientists (published by International Biographical Centre, Cambridge, England in 2004) in recognition of his achievements in the field of scientific research.

Contents

Preface

Multimedia as we know it has gained tremendous importance over the last decade. It spans quite a few areas of computer science involving programming, algorithms, communication technology, various media of communications and so on. It has raised the quality of communication by adding more than one media of communication such as audio, video, text, graphics and animation. Its importance in terms of medical science, engineering, entertainment, education, distance learning, and to all aspects of life, cannot be overstated. This book provides an up-to-date accounts of various research and developments taking place in this field of study,

In first chapter, we talk about communication network issues. Since a major concern of multimedia is quick and efficient flow of multimedia materials like audio and video, this chapter sets the scene. Network-on-Chip (NoC), which is considered as a global communication vehicle, is discussed. NetCal is a mathematical framework to derive worst-case bounds on maximum latency and backlog. With these two models, the delay and backlog buffer bounds can be calculated.

The next chapter discusses the problems of imparting distance learning through multimedia in developing countries. We suggest mobile technology as a viable and affordable media through which distance learning could be efficiently imparted to billions of people. We also present some examples of achievements in this field, such as the mobile use of telephone, photography, audio, video, internet, eBook, animations and so on, that could deliver effective distance education in developing countries.

The chapters go on to discuss the ubiquitous computing platform that should be designed for quality control of multimedia and data context through the Internet, as the standard of signals can be weaker based on geographical locations.

Next, image inpainting for Thangka images of Tibet is considered. Thangka images bear valuable cultural heritage of the region. A new method is proposed for damaged image inpainting of Thangka images; combining the shape of damaged patches and type of neighborhood patches according to the current algorithm characteristics of image inpainting, automaticaly implementing damaged regions. The chapter deals with the need of semantic-based Thangka image retrieval to establish an artifact annotation Thangka image database in a more object-oriented world. Thangka image annotation will be a heavy task with different classification, different content, and a picture with a lot of objects.

The next chapter discusses a web-based co-operative learning project between the Massachusetts Institute of Technology (MIT) in the USA and the Universidad Politécnica de Valencia (UPV) in Spain, which has been underway since 2000. Its aim is to put technological students in Valencia (Spain) and technological students in Boston (USA) in contact by means of a jointly developed interactive website. This website is an open platform that allows the registered students to interact with each other; building a technological social networking not only by using text-based messages (including a built-in chat facility), but also by uploading and downloading multimedia files, i.e. videos and graphics created by the students themselves. The content of the website is updated in real time and is fully developed and controlled by the participating students themselves, so as to reflect their interests, views and other cultural and social components.

The next chapter describes a mobile application for Android that has shown how a GPS-based social network can help people communicate between each other and display a map with information about important topics like road condition (traffic, checkpoints, car accidents, road work), Facebook events, Facebook Friends' position and any other event that can happen on a road. The main failure of current navigation applications is that traffic information is provided by sensors on the road, but users must pay to access them or must check them on a free website. The proposed application allows the user to have all the information he needs right on his mobile device and, according to Mobile Web 2.0 philosophy, the information is provided by the other social network users; a user can report an event that will be shown on other users' maps. This application can help reduce traffic jams and pollution. The application can ask the user for a traffic condition, if the user's speed is particularly slow and can notify the user of new events around him. According to privacy agreement the user can customize every aspect of the application, including notifications, requests, events visualization on his map and his own visualization on other users' map.

I express my sincere gratitude to InTech, Open Access publisher, for their help and guidance in this publication process, particularly to Ms Daria Nahtigal, Publishing Process Manager who was very helpful in getting things together for the book.

Dr. Sagarmay Deb
The University of Central Queensland,
Australia

Part 1

Efficient Flow of Multimedia Information Traffic

1

A Self-Similar Traffic Model for Network-on-Chip Performance Analysis Using Network Calculus

Yue Qian
School of Computer Science, National University of Defense Technology
China

1. Introduction

Since around year 2000, Network-on-Chip (NoC) has been proposed as a global communication paradigm to interconnect tens or hundreds of cores on a single chip (Bjerregaard & Mahadevan, 2006). One key challenge for NoCs has been Quality of Service (QoS), which is concerned about performance guarantees or bounds. To achieve QoS, formal performance analysis is essential because it overcomes the uncertainty in results and lengthiness in time of simulation-based approaches (Lu, 2007).

Network calculus (NetCal) (Chang, 2000; Cruz, 1991; Le Boudec & Thiran, 2004) is a mathematical framework to derive worst-case bounds on maximum latency and backlog. The beauty of NetCal relies on two abstraction models, an *arrival curve* for traffic, and a *service curve* for network elements (router, relay node, interface, channel, server etc.). Arrival curves bound the accumulated amount of traffic. Service curves describe minimal service levels of network elements. With these two models, the delay and backlog buffer bounds can be calculated. NetCal has been extremely successful when applied to ATM and IP networks with both differentiated and integrated services to achieve predictable performance without over-dimensioning network architectures (Le Boudec & Thiran, 2004). Recently NetCal has also been applied to wireless LAN (Agharebparast & Leung, 2005), sensor networks (Schmitt & Roedig, 2005), and on-chip networks (Qian et al., 2010) etc.

Our intention is to use NetCal for communication performance analysis of self-similar traffic in on-chip networks. ATM, Ethernet and Internet traffic has shown *self-similar* characteristics (Park & Willinger, 2000). In on-chip networks, it turns out also to be true for many applications, particularly, multimedia traffic, as supported by (Scherrer et al., 2005; Soteriou et al., 2006; Varatkar & Marculescu, 2004). By analyzing on-chip traffic traces, they demonstrate that packets injected from routing nodes possess scale-invariant burstiness over time. However, existing self-similar traffic models (Mao & Panwar, 2006; Park & Willinger, 2000) are not directly subject to NetCal analysis. The reason is simply because they do not comply with the arrival curve model. Therefore the purposes of our work are triple-folded: (1) to find an arrival curve for self-similar traffic, if it exists; (2) otherwise, propose an arrival curve to envelop the self-similar traffic; (3) to perform analysis based on the proposed arrival model using the NetCal framework. Performing these tasks should keep the beauty of NetCal and still enable us to apply known NetCal analysis methods and results to analyze the performance and buffering cost of networks transporting self-similar traffic flows.

The remainder of the chapter is organized as follows. Section 2 summarizes related work and our contributions. In Section 3, we first introduce the property of self-similar traffic. Then we present the Fractional Brownian Motion (FBM) model (Norros, 1995), which is used to characterize the self-similarity of traffic, and how to estimate FBM parameters. In Section 4, we present our main findings in the form of theorems, proposing an *extended arrival curve* to constrain self-similar traffic. Afterwards, in Section 5, we present formulas to calculate delay and backlog bounds. Assuming the latency-rate server model (Stiliadis & Varma, 1998) for network elements, we give closed-form equations. Moreover, to give a complete picture of our method, we describe a performance analysis flow to show how to conduct performance analysis for self-similar traffic. Experiments and results are reported in Section 6. Finally we draw conclusions in Section 7.

2. Related work

Since being initially identified in Ethernet by Leland et al. (Leland et al., 1994), traffic self-similarity has far-reaching influence on traffic modeling and performance analysis. Explorations of the nature of self-similarity and applications of this complex phenomenon have been extensively studied and summarized (Park & Willinger, 2000). In the context of NoCs, researchers have found the evidence of self-similarity from on-chip communication traces. In (Varatkar & Marculescu, 2004), Varatkar et al. first introduced self-similarity as a fundamental property exhibited by the bursty traffic between on-chip modules in multimedia video applications. This work captured the traffic characteristics between pair-wise nodes rather than for the entire network. Later, Soteriou et al. (Soteriou et al., 2006) empirically studied a large set of traffic traces gathered from the execution of SPEC, MediaBench and bit-parallel benchmarks over the entire on-chip network with different architectures and showed the presence of self-similar phenomena in on-chip traffic flows.

Cruz (Cruz, 1991) has pioneered the network calculus, which is based on bounds of traffic flows. A useful family of bound functions for concise descriptions has the form $\alpha(t) = rt + b$, where r is the rate and b limits the burstiness of the flow. Based on Cruz's foundation, Chang (Chang, 2000) and Le Boudec (Le Boudec & Thiran, 2004) have further developed the network calculus theory and based it on min-plus algebra. The basic elements in this algebra are arrival curves as an abstraction of application traffic and service curves as an abstraction for components (network elements). A well-defined service curve is the so-called latency-rate function $\beta_{R,T}$, where R is the service rate and T the maximum response delay of the node (Stiliadis & Varma, 1998).

Stochastic network calculus (Ciucu et al., 2005; Jiang, 2006; Starobinski & Sidi, 2000; Yin et al., 2002) is the probabilistic version of the (deterministic) network calculus. It has recently been developed for stochastic service guarantee analysis. Stochastic network calculus combines the deterministic network calculus with statistical multiplexing. For this, several stochastic versions of arrival curve have been proposed by extending the concept of arrival curve to the stochastic case based on the traffic amount property or virtual backlog property. Among the existing stochastic arrival curves, Sum of Exponentials, Weibull Bounded Burstiness (WBB), Fractional Brownian Motion (FBM) and Multifractal Brownian Motion (MBM) envelope processes consider the self-similar traffic (Mao & Panwar, 2006). In contrast to the deterministic arrival curves, stochastic arrival curves envelop traffic tighter but have higher implementation complexity.

In (Norros, 1995), Norros introduced the FBM model to capture the long-range dependence within the self-similar traffic. This model inspires WBB envelope process and is the basis for the FBM and MBM envelope processes (Mao & Panwar, 2006). Since the stochastic properties of the FBM process retain well when the traffic is multiplexed, randomly split, or goes through a buffering system, the FBM model serves well for the objective of concatenating single-hop analysis into an end-to-end analysis (Cheng et al., 2007).

We link self-similar traffic to deterministic network calculus. We develop an extended linear arrival model as its arrival curve, and then apply NetCal analysis on it. Our arrival curve is also constructed based on the FBM process. In contrast to other stochastic arrival curves, it is coupled with deterministic network calculus. Also, it is an extension of the traditional linear expression, thus easy to use and understand and simple in implementation. We summarize our contributions as follows:

- We prove that self-similar traffic cannot be enveloped by any deterministic arrival curve.
- We extend the linear arrival curve $\alpha_{r,b}(t) = rt + b$ with an excess probability ε as $\varepsilon\text{-}\alpha_{r,b}(t) = rt + b(\varepsilon)$, where ε reflects the probability of traffic burstiness surpassing its arrival curve. We prove that self-similar traffic can be characterized by the extended linear arrival curve $\varepsilon\text{-}\alpha_{r,b}$.
- Based on the extended self-similar traffic model, we derive delay and backlog bounds for self-similar traffic served by one or a series of concatenated network elements. Furthermore, we give closed-form equations to compute the bounds assuming the network elements are modeled by the latency-rate server (Stiliadis & Varma, 1998).
- We present a performance analysis flow starting from self-similar traffic and ending with results of delay and backlog bounds.

3. Self-similarity and FBM

In this section we give a definition of self-similar traffic (Park & Willinger, 2000), describe the FBM model (Fonseca et al., 2000; Norros, 1995), and introduce the estimation of FBM parameters, $(\bar{a}, \sigma, H)$ (Norros, 1995; Park & Willinger, 2000).

3.1 Self-similarity

Let $X(t)$ denote the traffic volume arriving in the tth time unit. Let $A(t)$ be the cumulative process indicating the total traffic volume from time 0 up to time t. $X(t)$ is also termed as the increment process of $A(t)$ as $X(t) = A(t) - A(t-1)$.

Given a stationary time series $X = (X(t),\ t = 1, 2, 3, ...)$, we define the m-aggregated series $X^{(m)} = (X^{(m)}(k),\ k = 1, 2, 3, ...)$ by summing the original series X over non-overlapping blocks of size m. The time series process X is called *asymptotically second-order self-similar* (as-s), if the autocorrelation function of $X^{(m)}$ and X follows

$$r^{(m)}(k) \sim r(k), \text{ as } m \to \infty,\ k \to \infty. \tag{1}$$

That is, at all scales the aggregated autocorrelation structures agree asymptotically to the autocorrelation structure of the entire series X.

The crucial feature of self-similar processes is that they exhibit *long-range dependence* (LRD). These LRD processes have an autocorrelation function $r(k)$ that decays with time lag k, i.e., $r(k) \sim k^{-\gamma}$ as $k \to \infty$, where $0 < \gamma < 1$. The *Hurst parameter* H is commonly used to measure the degree of LRD, and is related to the parameter γ by $H = 1 - \gamma/2$. In fact, with $1/2 < H < 1$, as-s and LRD imply each other, and self-similarity and LRD are often used interchangeably in practice.

3.2 FBM and its envelope process

Many different models are widely used to represent self-similarity. We use Fractional Brownian Motion (FBM) (Norros, 1995) to model the cumulative input traffic $A(t)$. The FBM input $\{A(t) : t \geq 0\}$ can be represented by

$$A(t) = \bar{a}t + \sigma Z(t), \tag{2}$$

where the mean arrival rate $E\{A(t)/t\} = \bar{a}$, and σ^2 is the variance of traffic in a time unit, and $\{Z(t) : t \geq 0\}$ is the standard (normalized) FBM process with Hurst parameter $H \in [1/2, 1)$.

The basic known property of FBM model is its marginal distribution (Norros, 1995), which allows computing an envelope process. For an FBM process $A(t)$ with mean $\bar{a}$ and variance σ^2, the envelope process $\hat{A}(t)$ can be defined as

$$\hat{A}(t) \stackrel{def}{=} \bar{a}t + k\sqrt{\sigma^2 t^{2H}} = \bar{a}t + k\sigma t^H, \tag{3}$$

where the parameter k determines the probability that $A(t)$ will exceed $\hat{A}(t)$ at time t as follows:

$$P\left(A(t) > \hat{A}(t)\right) = P\left(\frac{A(t) - \hat{a}t}{\sigma t^H} > k\right) = \varepsilon = \Phi(k), \tag{4}$$

where $\Phi(y)$ is the residual distribution function of the standard Gaussian distribution, using the approximation $\Phi(y) = \exp(-y^2/2)$, k is given by $k = \sqrt{-2\ln\varepsilon}$.

The FBM envelope process is advantageous: (1) It is parsimonious, i.e., only three parameters $(\bar{a}, \sigma, H)$ are required to completely characterize a self-similar source; (2) The input parameters $(\bar{a}, \sigma, H)$ can be estimated in real-time from the incoming traffic samples with minimal computational complexity (Fonseca et al., 2000).

3.3 Estimation of FBM parameters $(\bar{a}, \sigma, H)$

The FBM parameters $(\bar{a}, \sigma, H)$ can be estimated from a sample of traffic traces. To estimate $\bar{a}$ and σ, we first get the traffic cumulative process $A(t)$ from the sample. The mean arrival rate is derived as $\bar{a} = E\{A(t)/t\}$ and the variance of traffic in a time unit is given as $\sigma = \frac{\sqrt{\mathrm{Var}\{A(t)\}}}{t^H}$ (Norros, 1995).

To estimate Hurst parameter H, there are a number of methods: analysis of R/S (Range/Scale, rescaled adjusted range) statistic, analysis of the variance-time plot, the Whittle estimation and analysis based on wavelet function (Park & Willinger, 2000). We adopt the R/S method summarized as follows.

Given a sample of n observations in the time series (X_k, $k = 1, 2, ..., n$), the R/S statistic is denoted as $M\left[\frac{R(n)}{S(n)}\right] \sim cn^H$ as $n \to \infty$ and c is a positive constant. Taking the logarithm of the two parts gives $\log\left\{M\left[\frac{R(n)}{S(n)}\right]\right\} \sim H\log(n) + \log(c)$ as $n \to \infty$. Thus the H parameter can be estimated by placing the graph of the $\log\{M[R(n)/S(n)]\}$ on $\log(n)$ and using the obtained points to select a straight line with slope H based on the least-squares method (Park & Willinger, 2000).

4. Self-similar traffic model ε-$\alpha_{r,b}$

In Theorem 1, we prove that a self-similar traffic flow cannot be bounded by any deterministic function.

Theorem 1. *For a self-similar traffic flow, whose FBM envelope process is $\hat{A}(t) = \bar{a}t + k\sigma t^H$, there does not exist any wide-sense increasing deterministic function $\alpha(t)$ ($t > 0$) to envelope the flow.*

Proof. Using reduction ad absurdum, we assume there exists such $\alpha(t)$ for all $t > 0$ that $\alpha(t) \geq A(t)$, hence

$$P\{A(t) > \alpha(t)\} = 0, \tag{5}$$

where $A(t)$ denotes the cumulative function of the self-similar traffic flow. For any specified time t, the volume of $\alpha(t)$ is deterministic.

Since the self-similar flow is modeled by FBM, with the concept of the FBM envelope process, we can get $k = \sqrt{-2\ln\varepsilon}$ when $\varepsilon \to 0$, $k \to \infty$.

As $\bar{a}$ and σ are all positive and $t > 0$, there exists some $\varepsilon^* > 0$ which makes $k > \frac{\alpha(t)}{\sigma t^H}$, i.e., $\bar{a}t + k\sigma t^H > \alpha(t)$, at the same time, $P\{A(t) > \bar{a}t + k\sigma t^H\} = \varepsilon^*$.

Therefore

$$P\{A(t) > \alpha(t)\} > P\{A(t) > \bar{a}t + k\sigma t^H\} = \varepsilon^* > 0, \tag{6}$$

which conflicts Eq. (5). This means the condition can not be true, i.e., $\alpha(t)$ does not exist. □

Note that, in Theorem 1, $\alpha(t)$ covers any deterministic arrival curve, linear and nonlinear. However, in order to use NetCal theory for performance analysis of self-similar traffic, we develop in Theorem 2 an extended arrival curve for self-similar traffic, which is an ε-enhanced linear arrival curve.

Theorem 2. *For a self-similar traffic flow, whose FBM envelope process is $\hat{A}(t) = \bar{a}t + k\sigma t^H$, there exists a deterministic linear arrival curve ε-$\alpha_{r,b}(t) = rt + b(\varepsilon)$, having values exceeded by the traffic flow for any t with the upper excess probability $\varepsilon = \Phi(k)$, where $r > \bar{a}$, $b(\varepsilon) = (r-\bar{a})^{\frac{H}{H-1}}(\Phi^{-1}(\varepsilon)\sigma)^{\frac{1}{1-H}}H^{\frac{H}{1-H}}(1-H)$.*

Proof. Since the traffic flow exceeds the arrival curve ε-$\alpha_{r,b}$ with the upper excess probability ε ($0 < \varepsilon \leq 1$), we have

$$P\{A(t) > \varepsilon\text{-}\alpha_{r,b}(t)\} \leq \varepsilon = P\{A(t) > \hat{A}(t)\}, \tag{7}$$

hence

$$\varepsilon\text{-}\alpha_{r,b}(t) = rt + b(\varepsilon) \geq \hat{A}(t) = \bar{a}t + k\sigma t^{H}. \tag{8}$$

By Eq. (8) for all t, we get

$$(r - \bar{a})t - k\sigma t^{H} + b(\varepsilon) \geq 0. \tag{9}$$

Since the Hurst parameter $1/2 < H < 1$, Eq. (9) is satisfied for the stable case only $r - \bar{a} > 0$, therefore $r > \bar{a}$.

To proceed further it is sufficient to note that Eq. (9) has to be met for the worst case and therefore, the minimum value of the left side of Eq. (9) in turn must be equal to zero (as of a weak inequality).

Let $f(t) = (r - \bar{a})t - k\sigma t^{H} + b(\varepsilon)$, in order to compute the minimum value of $f_{\min}$, it is necessary to find t^* such that $\frac{df(t)}{dt} = 0$. Hence we have $(r - \bar{a}) - Hk\sigma t^{H-1} = 0$, t^* is given by $t^* = \left[\frac{k\sigma H}{(r - \bar{a})}\right]^{\frac{1}{1-H}}$.

Insert t^* into $f(t) = 0$, we get

$$\begin{aligned} b(\varepsilon) &= (\bar{a} - r)\left(\frac{k\sigma H}{r - \bar{a}}\right)^{\frac{1}{1-H}} + k\sigma\left(\frac{k\sigma H}{r - \bar{a}}\right)^{\frac{H}{1-H}} \\ &= (r - \bar{a})^{\frac{H}{H-1}}(\Phi^{-1}(\varepsilon)\sigma)^{\frac{1}{1-H}} H^{\frac{H}{1-H}}(1 - H). \end{aligned} \tag{10}$$

□

We can see that $b(\varepsilon)$ is a function of r ($r > \bar{a}$) and FBM parameters of $(\bar{a}, \sigma, H)$. Certainly, how closely the extended arrival curve constrains the traffic flow is sensitive to the excess probability ε, which is a measure of majorizing precision.

5. Performance analysis

Using the proposed arrival curve, we derive performance and backlog bounds based on the concepts of arrival and service curves (Le Boudec & Thiran, 2004).

5.1 General bounds

When a self-similar traffic flow with arrival curve $\varepsilon\text{-}\alpha_{r,b}$ is processed by a network element with service curve β, the maximum delay for the flow is bounded by:

$$D(\varepsilon\text{-}\alpha_{r,b}, \beta) = \sup_{t \geq 0}\{\inf\{\tau \geq 0 : \varepsilon\text{-}\alpha_{r,b}(t) \leq \beta(t + \tau)\}\}. \tag{11}$$

When a traffic flow is processed by a sequence of network elements, we could simply add the different maximum delays of each individual component together to obtain an end-to-end delay guarantee. However, in this case we can exploit the phenomenon known as Pay Bursts Only Once (Le Boudec & Thiran, 2004), and the end-to-end delay guarantee can be tightened by:

$$D(\varepsilon\text{-}\alpha_{r,b}, \beta_1 \otimes \beta_2 \otimes \ldots \otimes \beta_n). \tag{12}$$

The maximum buffer size that is required to buffer the traffic flow is bounded by:

$$B(\varepsilon\text{-}\alpha_{r,b}, \beta) = \sup_{t \geq 0}\{\varepsilon\text{-}\alpha_{r,b}(t) - \beta(t)\}. \tag{13}$$

And when the traffic flow traverses several consecutive elements, the total required buffer space can even be tightened by:

$$B(\varepsilon\text{-}\alpha_{r,b}, \beta_1 \otimes \beta_2 \otimes \ldots \otimes \beta_n). \tag{14}$$

Note that, strictly speaking, the delay and backlog "bounds" should be interpreted as "estimates" for maximum delay and backlog. Since the traffic is not entirely constrained by the arrival curve in our model due to ε, it is possible in theory that the calculated bounds may be exceeded, even though appearing only in extreme cases. However, to follow the terminology used in network calculus based performance analysis, we also use "bounds" for the estimated maximum delay and backlog in the chapter.

5.2 Bounds for latency-rate servers

In addition to the general performance bounds, we give equations to compute the bounds assuming the *latency-rate server* model for network elements (Stiliadis & Varma, 1998).

Consider a self-similar traffic flow with arrival model $\varepsilon\text{-}\alpha_{r,b}(t) = rt + b(\varepsilon)$ traversing a series of network elements, each element i ($i = 1, 2, 3, ..., n$) guarantees a latency-rate service curve $\beta_{R_i,T_i} = R_i(t - T_i)^+$, where R_i is the service rate and T_i delay to serve the flow. Notation $x^+ = x$, if $x \geq 0$; $x^+ = 0$, otherwise.

Let $R_{\min} = \bigwedge_{i=1}^{n} R_i$ and $T_{tol} = \sum_{i=1}^{n} T_i$. If $r \leq R_{\min}$, then the delay bound is

$$\begin{aligned} D(\varepsilon\text{-}\alpha_{r,b}, \beta_{R_1,T_1} \otimes \beta_{R_2,T_2} \otimes ... \otimes \beta_{R_n,T_n}) &= \frac{b(\varepsilon)}{R_{\min}} + T_{tol} \\ &= \frac{(r - \bar{a})^{\frac{H}{H-1}} (\Phi^{-1}(\varepsilon)\sigma)^{\frac{1}{1-H}} H^{\frac{H}{1-H}} (1 - H)}{\bigwedge_{i=1}^{n} R_i} + \sum_{i=1}^{n} T_i, \end{aligned} \tag{15}$$

and the buffer bound is

$$\begin{aligned} B(\varepsilon\text{-}\alpha_{r,b}, \beta_{R_1,T_1} \otimes \beta_{R_2,T_2} \otimes ... \otimes \beta_{R_n,T_n}) &= b(\varepsilon) + rT_{tol} \\ &= (r - \bar{a})^{\frac{H}{H-1}} (\Phi^{-1}(\varepsilon)\sigma)^{\frac{1}{1-H}} H^{\frac{H}{1-H}} (1 - H) + r\sum_{i=1}^{n} T_i. \end{aligned} \tag{16}$$

If $r > R_{\min}$, the bounds are infinite.

We can see when ε ($0 < \varepsilon \leq 1$) is approaching to 1, the backlog and delay bounds are deceasing. In particular, when ε equals 1, the value of $b(\varepsilon)$ will be zero and the delay and buffer bounds will equal to $\sum_{i=1}^{n} T_i$ and $r\sum_{i=1}^{n} T_i$, respectively. The reason is that, as ε increases,

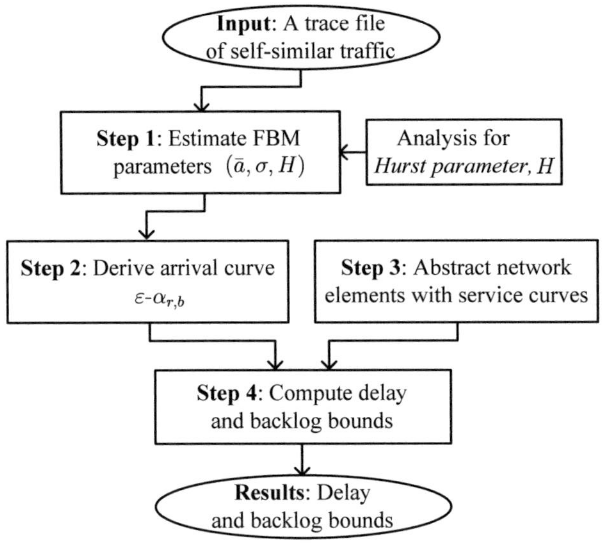

Fig. 1. Performance Analysis Flow Using Network Calculus on Self-Similar Traffic.

more bursty traffic exceeds the arrival curve. This is similar to the effect of lowering the traffic arrival curve. Thus the computed delay and backlog bounds become smaller.

5.3 Performance analysis flow

We illustrate the analysis flow in Figure 1. The input is a trace of self-similar traffic and output is delay and backlog bound results. The procedure contains four steps:

- Step 1: Estimate FBM parameters $(\bar{a}, \sigma, H)$ (Section 3.3). This step checks for self-similarity in the trace and performs, for example, the R/S analysis, to derive Hurst parameter H. With this step, we obtain its cumulative process.
- Step 2: Find its FBM envelope process, and further derive its ε-enhanced arrival model (Section 4).
- Step 3: Model network elements with service curves.
- Step 4: Compute delay and backlog bounds for its traversal through a single node or concatenated nodes. If the service models follow the latency-rate model, we can use the closed-form equations in Section 5.2 to compute the bounds.

6. Experiments and results

We devised experiments to (1) validate the proposed self-similar model; (2) show the correctness and tightness of calculated bounds via comparing them with simulated results. With the experiments, we also exemplify the performance analysis flow.

6.1 The simulation platform

We use a simulation platform in an open source simulation environment SoCLib (*SoCLib Simulation Environment*, n.d.) to collect application traces and to simulate their delay and backlog in on-chip networks.

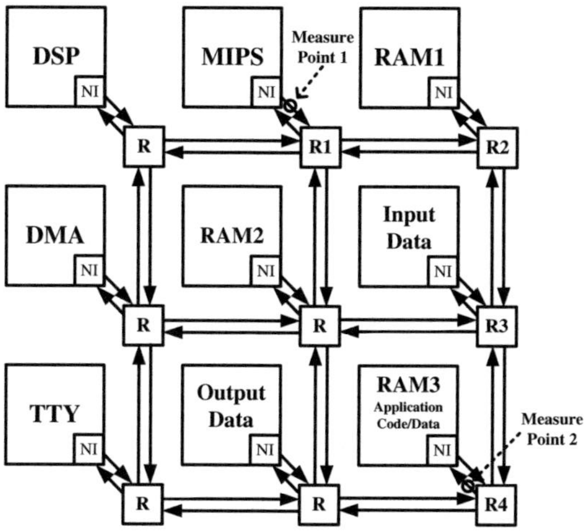

Fig. 2. The Simulation Platform.

As shown in Figure 2, the platform contains a MIPS R3000 processor, on-chip memories, a display component (TTY), and other components such as DSP and DMA. These components are interconnected with a 3×3 mesh network. The network performs wormhole flow control and uses XY routing. Routers are uniform, taking 5 cycles to deliver head flits and one cycle for other flits. Application code and data are stored in RAM3. The Network Interfaces (NIs) encapsulate transactions into flits and de-encapsulate flits into transactions.

We run four embedded multimedia programs on the MIPS: an MP3 audio decoder, an MPEG2 video decoder, a JPEG and a JPEG2000 decoder, respectively. The MP3 processes a 4KB audio stream, MPEG2 a 176×176 video frame, JPEG and JPEG2000 a 256×256 image. We set up two measurement points to observe the transactions between MIPS and RAM3 in the platform, as indicated in Figure 2. While application code running on the processor, at Point 1 we record the sequence number and timing of flits generated by MIPS in a trace file, and at Point 2 we observe the end-to-end delay experienced by each flit after traversing four routers, {R1, R2, R3, R4}, and the system backlog.

We have performed analysis and simulation for all the four application traces. For concise presentation, we only detail the analysis and simulation results of the MP3 application in Section 6.2 and Section 6.4, respectively. Section 6.3 discusses the derivation of the extended arrival curves for the MP3 application and the selection of parameters ε and r. Nevertheless, we report both analysis and simulation results on delay and backlog for all the applications in Section 6.5. For all results, the unit for delay is *cycle*, for backlog is *flit*. While examining traffic's self-similarity, we choose 100 cycles as the time window.

6.2 Analysis for MP3 application

The analysis of the MP3 application follows the four steps described in Section 5.3.

Step 1. The entire trace of MP3 application contains 1,697,249 flits in total and lasts for 46,696 hundreds of cycles as drawn in Figure 3. For such 100-cycle aggregated data series, we use the R/S analysis method to derive its Hurst parameter as illustrated in Figure 4. It turns out that H equals 0.86. This means the MP3 traffic exhibits good self-similarity. The FBM

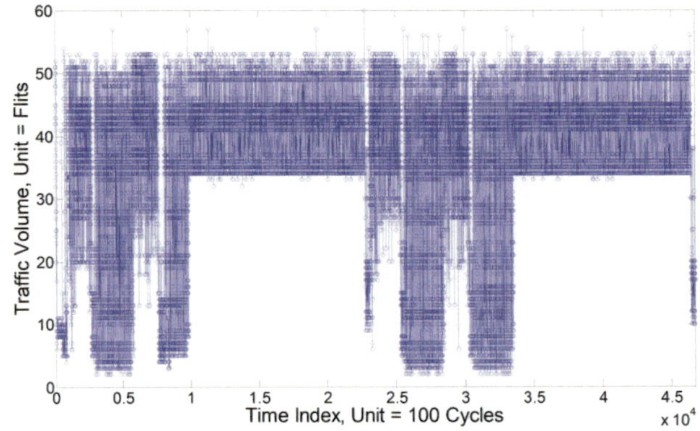

Fig. 3. Aggregated throughput trace obtained from the execution of MP3 application.

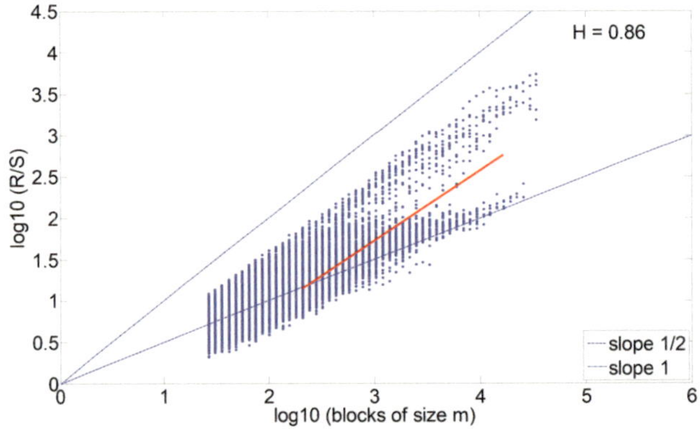

Fig. 4. Hurst Parameter Estimation via the R/S Method.

parameters of $\bar{a}$ and σ are also derived using the formulas presented in Section 3.3. We get the mean rate $\bar{a} = 36.35$ flits/100 cycles, and the variance in time unit of 100 cycles $\sigma = 0.33$.

Step 2. Assume the excess probability $\varepsilon = $ 1E-4 (1×10^{-4}), with derived $(\bar{a}, \sigma, H) = (36.35, 0.33, 0.86)$, we have the FBM envelope process $\hat{A}(t) = 36.35t + 1.417t^{0.86}$. Now we compute its extended arrival curve of ε-$\alpha_{r,b}$. Let $r = 37$ flits/100 cycles $> \bar{a}$, then with Eq. (10), we get $b(\varepsilon) = 10$ flits, thus ε-$\alpha_{r,b}(t) = rt + b(\varepsilon) = 37t + 10$.

Together with the MP3 cumulative process, the two curves of ε-$\alpha_{r,b}(t)$ and $\hat{A}(t)$ are plotted in Figure 5. As we can see, the derived model ε-$\alpha_{r,b}(t)$ tightly bounds the cumulative process of the self-similar traffic. This validates the correctness of our proposed self-similar arrival model.

Step 3. The routers are modeled as latency-rate servers with the same service curve of $\beta(t) = 100(t - 0.05)^+$, which represents that the routers delay head flits for 5 cycles and forward 100 flits per 100 cycles.

Step 4. Flits generated by MIPS passing through a tandem of routers {R1, R2, R3, R4} before arriving at RAM3. Using Eq. (15) and (16), in Section 5.2, the delay and backlog bounds can be calculated as 30 cycles and 17.4 flits, respectively.

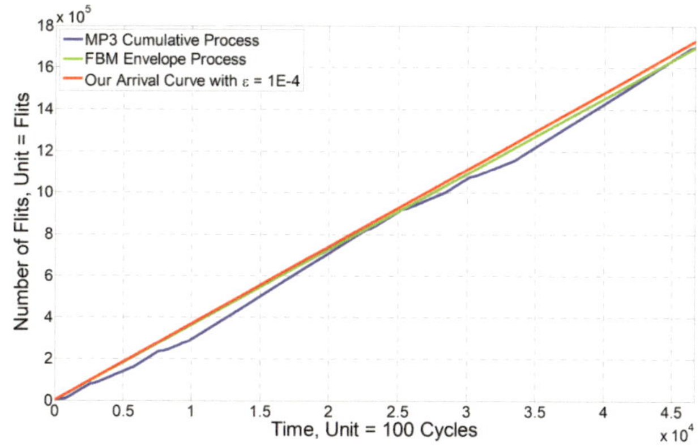

Fig. 5. Cumulative Process, FBM Envelope Process and ε-$\alpha_{r,b}$ Curve of Self-similar Traffic.

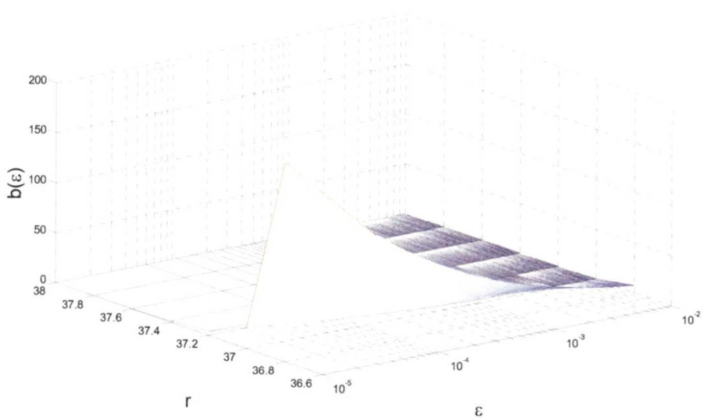

Fig. 6. $b(\varepsilon)$ with ε and r.

6.3 Discussions on extended arrival curves

6.3.1 Derivation of the extended arrival curves

For the MP3 application, we have obtained $(\bar{a}, \sigma, H) = (36.35, 0.33, 0.86)$. Using Equation 10, we get

$$b(\varepsilon) = 0.0554 \cdot (r - 36.35)^{-6.1429} \cdot (0.33 \cdot \sqrt{-2\ln\varepsilon})^{7.1429}. \tag{17}$$

This means that $b(\varepsilon)$ decreases as r or/and ε increases. The relation among b, r and ε is shown in the 3D Figure 6. With a small increase of r from 36.6 to 38, b is approaching 0. With an increase of ε, b is also decreasing and approaching to 0, but with a relatively less acceleration.

We also give the delay and backlog estimates as follows:

Delay Estimates:

$$D = 0.0554 \cdot (r - 36.35)^{-6.1429} \cdot (0.33 \cdot \sqrt{-2\ln\varepsilon})^{7.1429} + 20. \tag{18}$$

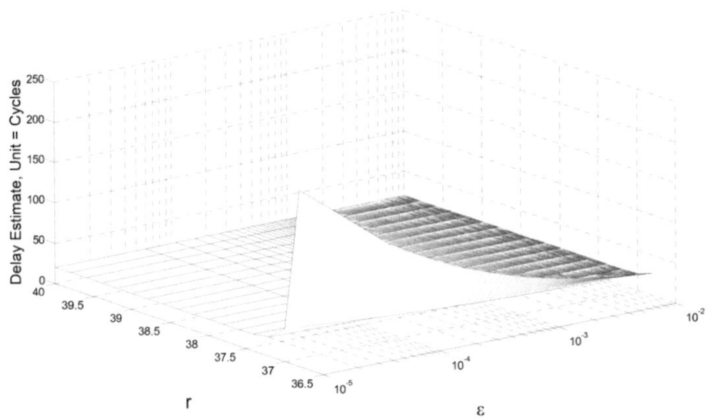

(a) Delay Estimates with ε and r

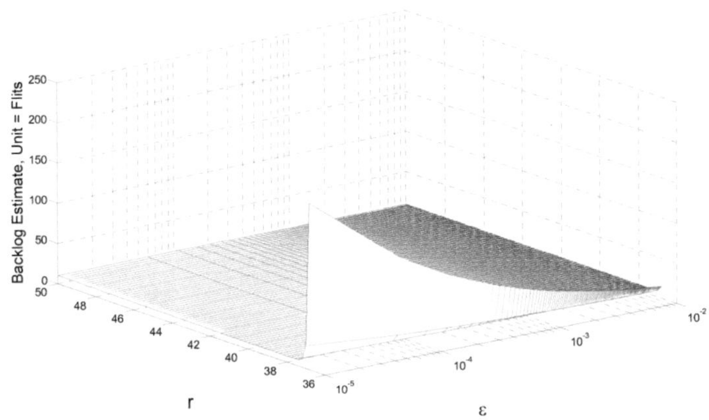

(b) Backlog Estimates with ε and r

Fig. 7. Delay and Backlog Estimates with ε, r.

Backlog Estimates:

$$B = 0.0554 \cdot (r - 36.35)^{-6.1429} \cdot (0.33 \cdot \sqrt{-2 \ln \varepsilon})^{7.1429} + 0.2 \cdot r. \quad (19)$$

From the formulas, we can see that D/B decreases as r or/and ε increases, in a similar way as $b(\varepsilon)$. We draw two 3D figures for the delay and backlog estimates in Figure 7. We can see that the three figures are similar in shape.

6.3.2 Selection of ε and r

As can be observed from Figure 6 and 7, the burstiness b, delay and backlog estimates (D and B) are very sensitive to the value of $r > 36.35$. Staring from $r = 36.5$, a small increase of r sharply reduces b, D and B. We choose $r = 37$, since, from this point, the curves do not go down quickly. With this value, we plot a 2D figure to show how the delay and backlog estimates vary with ε in Figure 8.

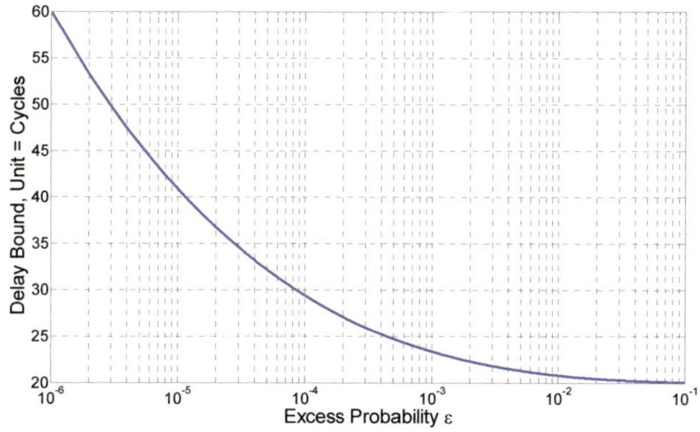

(a) Delay Bounds with Excess Probability ε

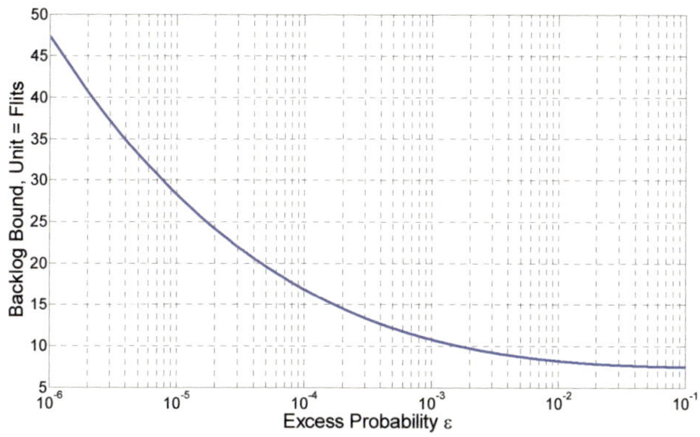

(b) Backlog Bounds with Excess Probability ε

Fig. 8. Delay and Backlog Bounds Affected by Excess Probability ε when $r = 37$ flits/100 cycles.

Figure 8 clearly shows that, as ε increases from 1E-6 to 1E-1, the delay and backlog are both decreasing and the decrease is sharp until ε goes beyond 1E-4. From then on, the decrement of ε affects the bounds lightly. For smaller ε, the arrival curve allows less flits excess, and the bounds are certainly calculated larger. "$\varepsilon = $ 1E-4 (1×10^{-4})" means that the tolerance of exceeding the arrival curve is one out of 10,000 flits. Note that the excess probability ε may come from application constraints. In such cases, ε is pre-determined and we only need to consider the relation between r and b.

With $\varepsilon =$ 1E-4, we can look closer on how the selection of rate r influences the delay and backlog estimates, as shown in Figure 9. While varying r from 36.8 to 38, both the delay and backlog estimates decrease and the decrease is sharp until r exceeds 37. From then on, the increase of r affects the bounds lightly. For smaller r, the burstiness b is greater so as to guarantee that the ε-$\alpha_{r,b}$ envelopes the traffic for a certain excess probability, and the bounds are consequently calculated larger. Since $r = 37$ is the turning point, we have chosen $r = 37$ for the MP3 application.

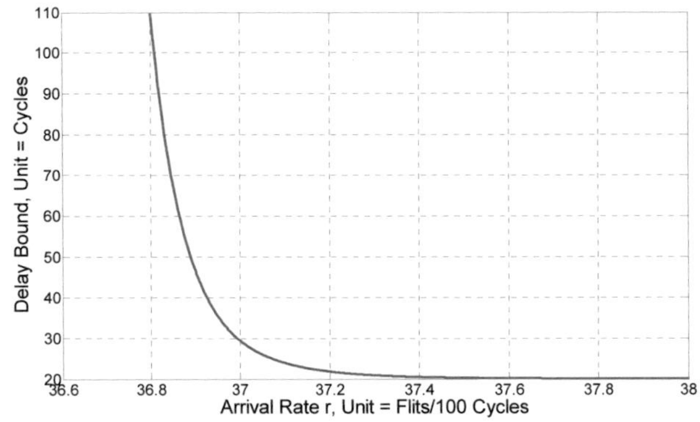

(a) Delay Bounds with Arrival Rate r

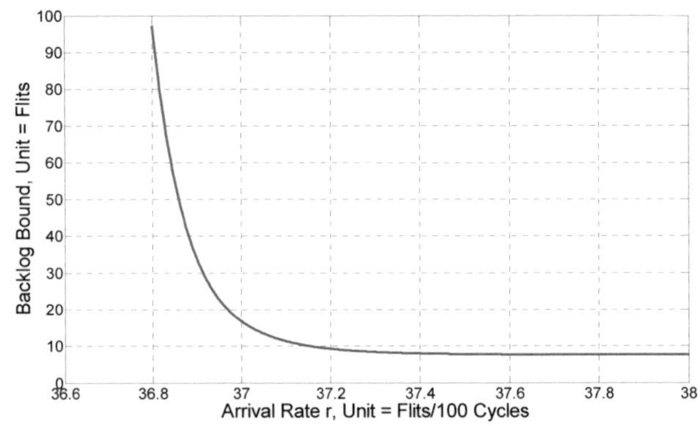

(b) Backlog Bounds with Arrival Rate r

Fig. 9. Delay and Backlog Bounds Affected by Arrival Rate r when $\varepsilon = 1\text{E-}4$.

6.4 Simulation results of MP3 application

We present detailed simulation results for the MP3 application.

Figure 10(a) plots the flit delay for a sequence of 1E+4 (1×10^4) flits. The calculated delay bound (30 cycles) is plotted as a straight line. We can see that there is no point above the line. Similarly, in Figure 10(b), for the sequence of 1E+4 flits, we plot the backlog value at each observing time point when a flit arrives at RAM3 and the calculated backlog bound (17.4 flits) as a straight line. We can see that there are some points above the line, indicating there exist some points beyond the bound caused by the burstiness of self-similar traffic. This in fact validates one finding in this chapter: no deterministic arrival curves can fully bound self-similar traffic.

Figures 11(a) and 11(b) show the delay and backlog histogram, respectively, for the entire trace. We find the maximum delay is 24 cycles and there are no flits experiencing larger delay than the bound of 30 cycles, so the excess ratio equals zero. For the backlog, the observed maximum backlog is 20 flits. There are 6 points in total exceeding the bound of 17.4 flits. The real exceeding ratio equals $6/1697249 = 3.53\text{E-}6$, which is far smaller than the assumed

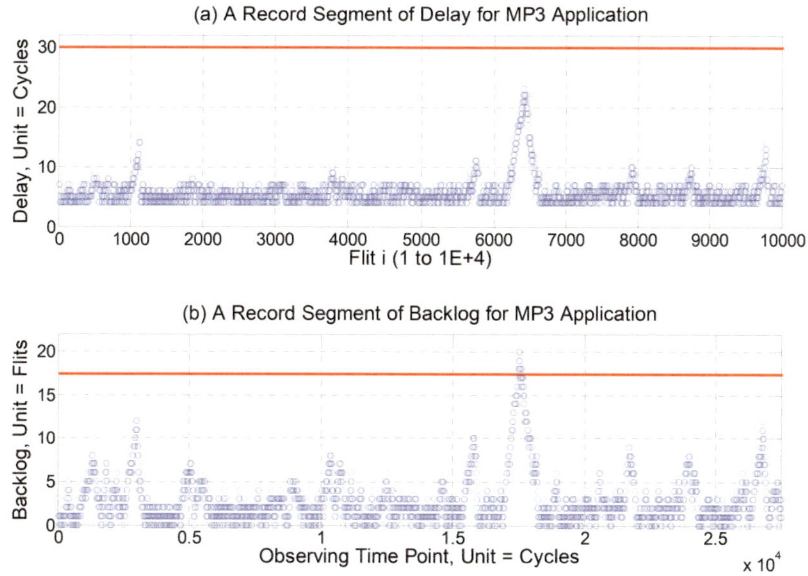

Fig. 10. Record Segment of Delay and Backlog for MP3 Application.

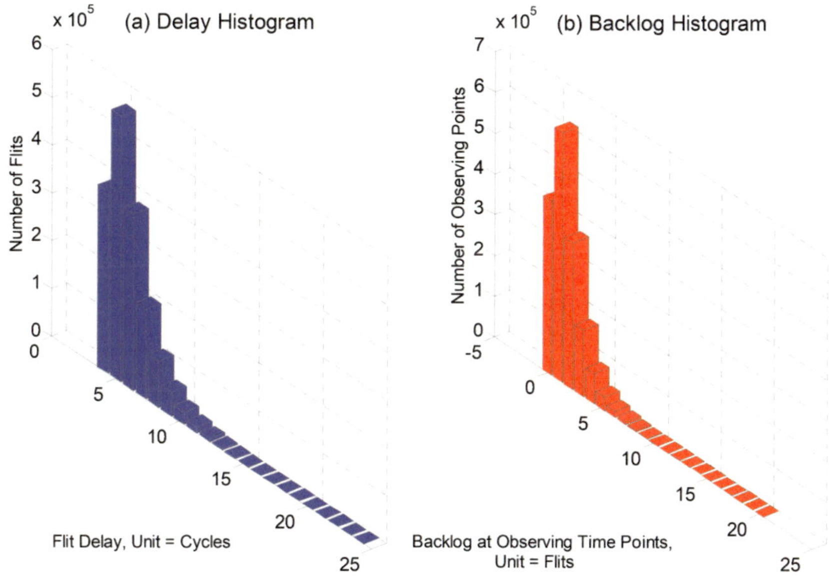

Fig. 11. Simulated Delay and Backlog Histograms for MP3 Application.

excess probability ε = 1E-4. This validates that our arrival curve with a predictive upper excess probability can well bound the self-similar traffic.

6.5 Summary of results for all applications

We summarize all calculated bounds and simulated results for the four applications, MP3, MPEG2, JPEG and JPEG2000 in Table 1, where we also list their FBM parameters and extended

Application	MP3	MPEG2	JPEG	JPEG2000
$\hat{a}$	36.35	25.06	38.32	34.51
σ	0.33	0.70	0.62	0.42
H	0.86	0.68	0.76	0.89
ε-$\alpha_{r,b}$ (ε=1E-4)	37t+10	26t+5	39t+6	35t+12
D	30	24.77	26.23	32.49
D_s	24	20	22	29
ϵ_D	0	0	0	0
B	17.4	9.98	14.09	19.59
B_s	20	13	17	24
ϵ_B	3.53E-6	4.47E-6	1.04E-6	2.61E-6

Table 1. Calculated and Simulated Results for MP3, MPEG2, JPEG and JPEG2000

arrival curves. We denote calculated delay bound and maximum simulated delay as D and D_s, respectively, and calculated backlog bound and maximum simulated backlog as B and B_s, respectively. The ϵ_D and ϵ_B represent the calculated exceeding ratio of the points beyond the delay and backlog bound, respectively. From this table, we can see that all the calculated delay bounds well constrain the simulated delay, i.e., $\epsilon_D = 0$. The calculated backlog bounds fail to constrain the maximum observed backlog in simulations. This results in $\epsilon_B > 0$, but we can observe $\epsilon_B << \varepsilon$. This means the proposed arrival models are good.

7. Conclusion

Performance analysis techniques must properly characterize traffic flows. In this chapter, we have presented a traffic arrival model for self-similar traffic, which is a very influential category of traffic observed in various networks. This model complies with the linear arrival model, and enhances it with an additional parameter, excess probability ε, to capture the probability of bursty traffic surpassing the linear arrival envelope. We develop such a model because of two reasons. One is that, as we have proved in the chapter, self-similar traffic cannot be bounded by any deterministic function. The other is that we hope to keep the elegance of the traffic abstraction in network calculus. With such an ε-enhanced arrival curve, we have shown how to apply network calculus theory for performance analysis of self-similar traffic flows. Assuming the latency-rate server model, we give closed-form equations for computing delay and backlog bounds for self-similar traffic traversing a tandem of network elements. We have also devised experiments to exemplify the performance analysis flow. Our simulations with real on-chip multimedia application traces have validated our model and results.

We have aimed our performance analysis of self-similar traffic for on-chip networks. However, the arrival-curve-compliant self-similar traffic model and its associated performance analysis method and formulas are equally applicable to off-chip networks, since we do not make any NoC-specific assumptions. Nevertheless, we believe our approach is most beneficial to the design of NoCs since NoC is a closed system focusing on specific application domains whereas traffic can be closely inspected, properly profiled and characterized.

8. References

Agharebparast, F. & Leung, V. C. M. (2005). Modeling wireless link layer by network for efficient evaluations of multimedia QoS, *Proceedings of IEEE International Conference on Communications*, Vol. 2, pp. 1256–1260.

Bjerregaard, T. & Mahadevan, S. (2006). A survey of research and practices of network-on-chip, *ACM Computing Survey* Vol. 33(No. 1): 1–51.

Chang, C.-S. (2000). *Performance Guarantees in Communication Networks*, Springer-Verlag.

Cheng, Y., Zhuang, W. & Ling, X. (2007). Towards an FBM model based network calculus framework with service differentiation, *Mobile Networks and Applications* Vol. 12(No. 5): 335–346.

Ciucu, F., Burchard, A. & Liebeherr, J. (2005). A network service curve approach for the stochastic analysis of networks, *Proceedings of the 2005 ACM SIGMETRICS*, pp. 279–290.

Cruz, R. L. (1991). A calculus for network delay, part I: Network elements in isolation and part II: Network analysis, *IEEE Transactions on Information Theory* Vol. 37(No. 1): 114–141.

Fonseca, N., Mayor, G. & Neto, C. (2000). On the equivalent bandwidth of self-similar sources, *ACM Transactions on Modeling and Computer Simulation* Vol. 10(No. 2): 104–124.

Jiang, Y. (2006). A basic stochastic network calculus, *Proceedings of the 2006 ACM SIGCOMM*.

Le Boudec, J.-Y. & Thiran, P. (2004). *Network Calculus: A Theory of Deterministic Queuing Systems for the Internet*, Number 2050 in LNCS, Springer-Verlag.

Leland, W. E., Taqqu, M. S., Willinger, W. & Wilson, D. V. (1994). On the self-similar nature of ethernet traffic (extended edition), *IEEE/ACM Transactions on Networking* Vol. 2(No. 1): 1–15.

Lu, Z. (2007). *Design and analysis of on-chip communication for network-on-chip platforms*, Ph.D. thesis, Royal Institute of Technology.

Mao, S. & Panwar, S. S. (2006). A survey of envelope processes and their applications in quality of service provisioning, *IEEE Communications Surveys and Tutorials* Vol. 8(No. 3): 2–20.

Norros, I. (1995). On the use of fractal brownian motion in the theory of connectionless networks, *IEEE Journal on Selected Areas in Communications* Vol. 13(No. 6): 953–962.

Park, K. & Willinger, W. (2000). *Self-similar Network Traffic and Performance Evaluation*, John Wiley and Sons.

Qian, Y., Lu, Z. & Dou, W. (2010). Analysis of worst-case delay bounds for on-chip packet-switching networks, *IEEE Transactions on Computer-Aided Design of Integrated Circuits and Systems* Vol. 29(No. 5).

Scherrer, A., Fraboulet, A. & Risset, T. (2005). Analysis and synthesis of cycle-accurate on-chip traffic with long-range dependence, *Technical report 2005-53, LIP, ENS-Lyon* .

Schmitt, J. & Roedig, U. (2005). Sensor network calculus - a framework for worst case analysis, *Proceedings of the International Conference on Distributed Computing in Sensor Systems*, pp. 141–154.

SoCLib Simulation Environment (n.d.). On-line, available at http://www.soclib.fr/.

Soteriou, V., Wang, H. & Peh, L. (2006). A statistical traffic model for on-chip interconnection networks, *Proceedings of IEEE International Symposium on Modeling, Analysis, and Simulation of Computer and Telecommunication Systems (MASCOTS'06)*.

Starobinski, D. & Sidi, M. (2000). Stochastically bounded burstiness for communication networks, *IEEE Transactions on Information Theory* Vol. 46(No. 1): 206–212.

Stiliadis, D. & Varma, A. (1998). Latency-rate servers: A general model for analysis of traffic scheduling algorithms, *IEEE/ACM Transactions on Netwroking* Vol. 6(No. 5): 611–624.

Varatkar, G. & Marculescu, R. (2004). On-chip traffic modeling and synthesis for mpeg-2 video applications, *IEEE Transactions of Very Large Scale Integration (VLSI) Systems* Vol. 12(No. 1).

Yin, Q., Jiang, Y., Jiang, S. & Kong, P. Y. (2002). Analysis on generalized stochastically bounded bursty traffic for communication networks, *Proceedings of the 27th IEEE Conference on Local Computer Networks (LCN'02)*.

2

Ubiquitous Control Framework for Delivering Perceptual Satisfaction of Multimedia Traffic

K. L. Eddie Law[1] and Jacek Ilow[2]
[1]*Kirin Cloud Solutions, Ltd.*
[2]*Dalhousie University*
[1]*Hong Kong*
[2]*Canada*

1. Introduction

With the latest computing technology, people can store information including audio, video, and data on the Internet. And the advanced networking protocol designs can easily enable interactive communications among users, applications, and services through wireless tablets and mobile devices (Satyanarayanan, 2001). However, people like to connect to the Internet while moving, the connectivity may vary during the course of an active session of a user. Although many portable device can provide high-speed connectivity, a user may move into area with weak signal or thin bandwidth, which possibly hinder the reception of satisfactory multimedia traffic. In today's business, it is important to make sure the satisfaction of content subscribers. Thus, it is adamant to develop a ubiquitous control framework to offer perceptual satisfaction of multimedia subscribers.

The ubiquitous computing platform should be designed for quality control of multimedia and data context through the Internet. The framework should manage the network and computing resources, such that the delivered information should at least meet the expected minimal perceptual quality of multimedia traffic stream of an end-user. In this chapter, a few basic design parameters for justifying the performance and design of the control framework will be elaborated. Quantitatively, different Quality of Service (QoS) parameters, e.g., packet loss rate, have been widely used for session transmission control. But for visual evaluation, the terminology known as Quality of Experience (QoE) has recently been widely used. QoE is a measure of performance expectations of the end-user; it may augment QoS by providing the quantitative link to user perception. Indeed, the only way to know how customers see your business is to look at it through their eyes.

Nowadays, due to the widespread use of mobile devices, the rapidly increasing demand on network resources impacts the underlying investment on high-performance hardware devices, which then affects the cost of a network architecture. Then, on the other hand, higher visual quality can then impact the number of subscribers and subsequently the top line income of a networking firm. As a result, a good visual quality control system with effective utilization of network resources for a networking firm is desirable. In the following, we shall elaborate the QoS and QoE design issues. Then a multimedia control framework will be proposed to offer satisfactory perceptual to ubiquitous multimedia subscribers. Its improvements will be thoroughly discussed.

2. Visual metrics and control frameworks

2.1 Measuring metrics

From the signal processing algorithmic design, multimedia sessions may consist of voices, images, videos, and data. Different signal types use different encoding/decoding algorithms for storage and transmissions. For example, MPEG (Motion Picture Experts Group) is a family of standards used for coding audio-visual information, e.g., movies, video, music, in a digital compressed format. The JPEG (Joint Photographic Experts Group), GIF (Graphic Image File), BMP (bitmap) are examples of image encoding data formats. Among them, bitmap image takes more memory spaces with sharper imaging quality because it has 256 quantization levels for each of the three base colors. An JPEG image is coded with a lossy Discrete Cosine Transform (DCT). It uses less memory space with a lower visual quality.

Peak signal-to-noise ratio (PSNR) is an easy-to-use error measurement metric, and is widely used for providing quantitative evaluation of receiving multimedia quality. Indeed, the PSNR ratio is more or less a subjective measurement technique, and it may fail to reflect what appear in images. As shown in Fig. 1, two images with identical PSNRs. But the one shown in Fig. 1(b) appears to give inferior visual quality (Winker & Mohandas, 2008). This is due to the local accumulation of errors on some nearby pixels. With the nonlinear functionality of retina in human vision system, the perceived quality can be drastically misleading. With the errors spread evenly across all pixels in the image, the one shown in Fig. 1(a) may be considered with better encoded quality.

(a) (b)

Fig. 1. Human vision system and images with identical PSNRs (Winker & Mohandas, 2008).

As a result, PSNR may not be able to reflect the visual perceptual quality of multimedia content. That is, some perceptually poor and appealing images may have identical PSNRs (Grega et al., 2008). At this current moment, there is no conclusive measure that should be commonly accepted as the right measure for quantifying QoE. Hence, the Mean Opinion Score (MOS) is then recommended by the International Telecommunication Union (ITU) (ITU-T Recommendation P.800, 1996). It is a subjective measure, and a number of users should rate the quality using a five-point scale from 1 to 5, inclusively, as listed in Table 1. The MOS is the arithmetic mean of all individual scores for judging the quality of a delivering video.

MOS	Quality	Perception
5	Excellent	Imperceptible
4	Good	Perceptible
3	Fair	Slightly annoying
2	Poor	Annoying
1	Bad	Very annoying)

Table 1. Mean Opinion Score (MOS).

Then from the perspective of network architectural design, the quality of a transmission session through the Internet is usually characterized by the term Quality of Service (QoS) using parameters, such as packet loss rate, transmission bandwidth, queue length, jitter, and delay etc. Each of these parameters can be used for performance analysis. Currently, there are a few standardized QoS associated network designs, for example, the Differentiated Service (Blake et al., 1998) system model through the recommendation of the Internet Engineering Task Force (IETF). In general, network operators have to monitor and manage network resources properly in order to deal with network congestion problems and packet loss issues so as to meet different QoS requirements. Network-introduced errors may be the sources of decoded signal errors. For example, as observed from the two rugby team pictures shown in Fig. 2, both of them suffer identical overall loss conditions in networks. The errors are spread across all pixels in Fig. 2(a) which gives a more appealing appearance. However, the errors are localized in Fig. 2(b), which may irritate the acceptance of a subscriber.

(a) (b)

Fig. 2. Network condition: 1% packet loss rate, 10 ms delay, 50 μs jitter, 500 kbps bandwidth (Winker & Mohandas, 2008).

Through these observations, QoE and QoS may be related but not in a linear way. What can be the proper way to assert the quality of online multimedia service? Objective evaluation methods are simpler because user inputs are usually not required. For example, data can be retrieved from network-level measurements, e.g., packet loss rate, or media-level measurements, e.g., PSNR, as the input for quality assessment. However, as discussed, they may not be able to judge delivered multimedia quality.

The subjective method using MOS for QoE can be a feasible solution. However, each subscriber may give a completely different MOS result. Furthermore, the same person under emotional stress can give a completely different score. As a result, we can consult some nonlinear functional methods for judging delivering visual quality. And some parameters are not considered in these methods. For example, the loss of volume is not considered by the Perceptual Evaluation of Speech Quality (PESQ), which is recommended by the ITU for determining the quality of a speech signal, in order to make the model tractable. Also, the latency between viewers and the video is not considered in Video Quality Measurement (VQM) model (Rajagopalan, 2010). Higher-order variations, i.e., the burstiness, of end-to-end delay and loss are not considered in many models for assessing VoIP quality.

Similar to PESQ, there are a few subjective methods that can assist in judging visual quality. One of the them is called Visual Differences Predictor (VDP). It is used to characterize the retina response curve. Although the computation complexity is relatively high, it can be used for quantifying image quality based on a reference image. Details of the VDP design can be found in Appendix A.

2.2 Examples of quality control frameworks

There are some basic architectural designs (Agarwal et al., 2008; Huang et al., 2008; Lum & Lau, 2002) for serving multimedia traffic adaptively according to varying network condition. The common goal is to improve the visual quality of multimedia traffic at recipients. In (Lum & Lau, 2002), proxy server or intermediate network server is used to relay and re-adapt information content for changed networking condition. As of today, there are a large amount of proxy video servers deployed across the Internet today. However, most of these proxies are for relay purpose only.

As reported in (Agarwal et al., 2008), a controlled testbed for experimenting video traffic delivery using peer-to-peer (P2P) streaming has been used. The results have indicated that tested P2P streaming systems carry significant overhead (up to 35% over the video stream size) with an average start-up delay of about 11 sec. Besides, an additional video buffering time of 30 sec is needed to combat packet arrival jitters for video playback. Despite these drawbacks, the P2P systems are robust regarding peer churn, and generate larger captured P2P bandwidth than using an over-provisioned server. Furthermore, they have found that quantitative measure such as PSNR, which is used among many P2P video streaming research reports, can not properly reflect the QoE.

Another investigation on P2P streaming can be found in (Huang et al., 2008). The paper offers a generic design framework, and identifies different building blocks in a system, for example, the file segmentation strategy, replication strategy, content discovery and management, piece/chunk selection policy, transmission strategy and authentication. The goal is to achieve a scalable system with efficient replication strategies for offering user-level satisfaction. A new fluency index has then been introduced as a performance measure for evaluating the health of the systems and the user satisfaction. Typically, the index measures the fraction of time a user spent watching a movie with respect to the total time spent on both the waiting and watching times. This design closely relies on the underlying network performance, instead of attempting to interpret and serve different types of content information. That is, the accuracy of the fluency index regarding perceptual quality has not been examined in the paper.

Then in (Law & Leung, 2003), a set of application programming interfaces (APIs) has been designed for programmable nodes in networks. This implies nodes on the Internet can function together in the form of loosely-coupled computing devices. This indicates that adaptation of traffic can be made inside the Internet. But the operation details for programs to execute must be carefully controlled by network and content service providers. In general, overlay networks provide better security control to network providers and code distribution flexibility to application providers. However, the response times may be slightly longer than those with programmable node concepts. For example, BitTorrent is one simple broadcasting mechanism for code distribution across end-users' computers, which operate as virtual network servers. To advance the design, structured overlays, such as using Distributed Hash Tables (DHTs) (Stoica et al., 2001), can be used.

In (Chen et al., 2009), a proposed framework with QoE consideration known as `OneClick` is proposed. Its operations is trivial. The client informs the server system directly regarding receiving perceptual quality. Upon viewing the multimedia content, when a user finds the receiving quality of content annoying, he or she can click certain button repeatedly to indicate his or her dissatisfaction. Therefore, a session with a larger number of clicks indicates a poorer receiving perceptual quality. The `OneClick` design can be considered as a reciprocal of Mean Opinion Score (MOS) (ITU-T Recommendation P.800, 1996). The `OneClick` may offer real-time response to the server system, although it has not been examined (Chen et al., 2009).

3. Multimedia agent framework

A network infrastructure is shown in Fig. 3. Initially the traffic communicating between a mobile client C and service provider S is traveling over the Path 1 as shown. Upon moving, the client C may have arrived at another location, and the communicating path has been switched to Path 2. The associated networking parameters might have completely changed, for example, the bottleneck link bandwidth and propagation delay, etc. As a result, the amount of data flow and traveling latency could be completely different, which can then impact the perceptual quality of receiving multimedia traffic.

Our proposed quality control framework is called Multimedia Agent Framework (MAF). The goal is to adapt traffic content to changing network constraints dynamically. The foundation of the framework is based on agent technology. A few basic components are defined for the system to operate properly. In Fig. 3, a functional connection is consisted of at least a content provider S, a mobile client C, and two agents, which sit at the edges on the Internet. Depending on the direction of the traffic flow, the agents are generically named the Ingress Agent (IA) and Egress Agent (EA). For the depicted traffic flow from a server to a client, the agents connecting to the source and destination are called ingress agent and egress agent,

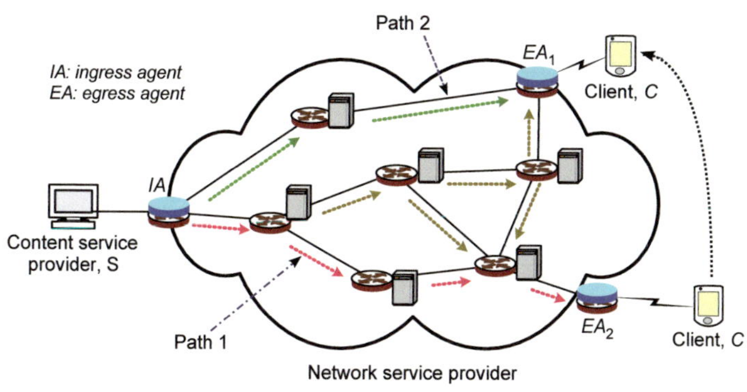

Fig. 3. An operating model of the multimedia agent framework.

respectively. Since wireless connections are not always stable, a mobile client may encounter different perceptual experiences while traveling. For example, the access bandwidth between C and egress agent EA_2 is 54 Mbps for 802.11g, while the one between C and EA_1 can be 11 Mbps for 802.11b. And in this paper, we assume that the bottleneck always occurs at the wireless link between egress agent and client.

To sustain a satisfactory user experience of a mobile client under changing networking conditions, traffic context can be adjusted accordingly (Banavar & Bernstein, 2002; Noble, 2000; Lum & Lau, 2002) through the proposed quality control framework. Apart from the ingress and egress agents, the framework allows content alternation within the Internet upon permitted by both the content service providers and subscribers. But at the current stage, we focus on the basic operating model which functions between the two agents.

3.1 Communication model

A traditional client-server transaction model is shown in Fig. 4(a). Suppose that a client tries to retrieve a web page, which is consisted of one HTML text document, and one picture file. Two separate HTTP GET requests from the client can be used to obtain the two files from the server. But in multimedia agent framework, a high-level conceptual design feature is enabled through the two agents, as shown in Fig. 4(b). Upon receiving the HTTP GET request from client, the egress agent also delivers information regarding the associated resource constraint of the wireless link to the ingress agent. Then the ingress agent can represent the client to collect both files and examine if the latest available resources are sufficient to receive both files in perfect condition. If not, the ingress agent can adjust the file context to meet the latest available QoS constraints for the client.

To have the framework worked as expected, structural control message flows between the egress and ingress agents have been designed. And these control messages are called "capsules" messages. In order to create a lightweight and effective design, multiple operating phases are introduced, which include: initialization, QoS negotiation, and provision phases. When a client moves from one access point to another access point, packets may be lost temporarily due to incorrect routing. This error can be reduced if the path change indication can be saved within the Internet. At the moment, this layer 3 operation is not investigated in this paper. Our current focus is on the changes of resource constraints, whereas multimedia information may not be able to provide the expected quality at the recipient.

For a newly moving-in mobile user, an egress agent may not be aware of any existing active connections. It starts to take notice, if this client sends a new request, retransmits a request, or the agent receives an incoming redirected messages from a server through the mobile IP protocol (Perkins, 2002; Johnson et al., 2004; Law & Lau, 2010). In either of these cases, the egress agent should start an initialization phase. That is, the egress agent attempts to establish and register a relationship with the corresponding ingress agent. The next stage is to begin a negotiation phase. At the current stage, the information being passed between the agents is for QoS monitoring. This enables the ingress agent to make decision on service class selection with an estimated performance for a specific traffic type. In future, information regarding service subscription should be integrated. This indicates that the right of use of a service class must also be verified if it is covered in its paid services. Then afterward, based on measured QoS parameters, the ingress agent makes decision if any modifications should be applied to the traffic, which should be delivered with satisfaction expectation of the subscriber. The role

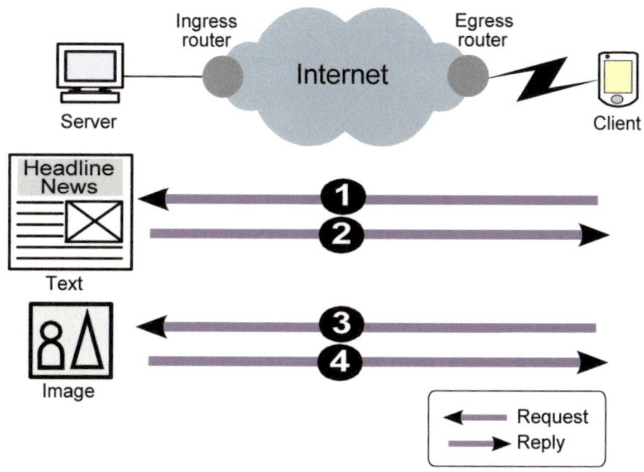

(a) Traditional client-server model.

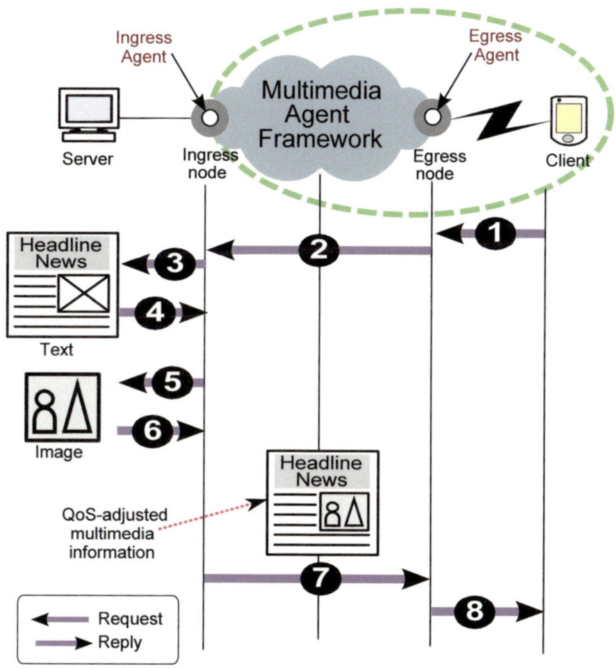

(b) Conceptual model of multimedia agent framework.

Fig. 4. Network transaction models for multimedia traffic.

of QoS monitoring plays an important role in determining the method of adaptations which should be carried out.

With the ubiquity of wireless devices, browsers have been the common tools for accessing different information on the Internet. It becomes naturally and important that the multimedia agent framework should start extending the protocol into REpresentational State Transfer (RESTful) model in future.

3.2 Delivering content adaptation

The multimedia agent framework can tailor the content to meet the QoE expectations of subscribers. At the moment, content adaptations are carried out at the edges of the Internet, i.e., the ingress and egress agents. The adaptation should depend on the business contract between content and network providers, which may be outside the scope of this chapter. Collectively, we call these nodes the adaptation nodes. For carrying out meaningful operations in these nodes, then a number of information must be learnt and communicated among the ingress and egress agents. As shown in Fig. 5, the types of information should include: 1) user's QoE expectations, 2) properties of content material, 3) latest network status, 4) available network access interfaces of devices.

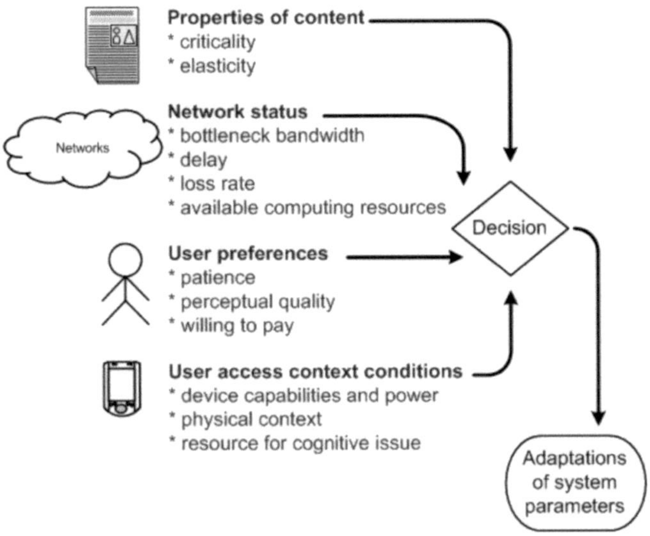

Fig. 5. Decision parameters.

3.3 User preferences and expectation

In order for the infrastructure to work seamlessly and meet the QoEs of subscribers, their preferences and expectations should be set at the initial phases and passed back to the content providers. The associated agents can obtain this information for adaptation purpose, if needed. There are certainly other methods available for this type of information retrieval, e.g., the Service Level Agreement (SLA) through policy-based management. The capability description can follow the defined syntax structure, such as the Composite Capability/Preference Profile (CC/PP) from World-wide Web Consortium (W3C), or Media Feature Sets from IETF.

Some parameters can assist the network to adapt to the QoE expectation of the multimedia traffic:

- Does a subscriber want the content to be retrieved as quickly as possible?
  - In video streaming, significant variations in delivery time result in jerky video and choppy audio. The resulting video has a lower QoE value than a smoothly playback video.
- Does the subscriber want the critical content to be retrieved unfailingly?
  - Ranking or priority of content may be desirable.

For multimedia information, more thorough query should be carried out. Questions may have to be asked regarding, for example, the acceptable choices for picture sizes and compression granularities, etc. These collected data can then be combined into a set of meta-information.

3.4 Content: meta-information

The purpose of having meta-information in the setting is to assist all components in the framework to parse and retrieve desired parameters as quickly as possible. For data files, meta-information may contain file size, version, title, language, and authors. For multimedia content, additional meta-information may include minimal required and desired transmission bit rates, display size, compression ratio, and encoding methods. These extra data can assist the adaptation agents to carry out appropriate operations, if needed. Extensible Markup Language (XML) can be a possible choice for embedding the meta-information regarding the requirements of services and QoEs of subscribers.

3.5 Network status

In general, it is common to characterize a network path between two end-systems using available channel bandwidth, end-to-end delay (or round-trip delay), and packet loss rate. With adaptation capability, computation power can be added to indicate if an adaptation node can handle a large number of connections simultaneously. The agents in network may offer computation services for information being delivered from a sender to a receiver. These parameters are the traditional network layer QoS parameters.

3.5.1 Delays and available resources

For the framework to operate smoothly, we should establish methods to measure available resources in the networks. For example, in a client-server model, packets from server are relayed from one node to other until they reach the egress node that the client is connecting to. In the following, we examine different delay components incurred along the network infrastructure. A packet has to spend times and delays while traveling through nodes and links along the path, respectively. The delay components are additive, and the aggregate delay across the networks is the summation of delay values in various nodes and connecting links. Typically, four different types of delays are introduced in networks:

- Propagation delay, f_{G_i}, for a link i;
- Transmission delay, $f_T(s, B)$, for packet size s and available bandwidth B;
- Processing delay, $f_C(c_p, c_b, s)$, where c_p for incoming packet processing, c_b for outgoing interface determination given a packet with size s;
- Queuing delay, f_{Q_j}, for the queue at node j.

The total one-way delay across the networks is the summation of all these delay components of all nodes and links along a path, as shown in (1). With these parameters, other network characteristics such as bandwidth and computation power can be implicitly reflected in the transmission and processing delay components, respectively.

$$T_D = \sum_{i=1}^{m} \left(f_{T_i}(s, B_i) + f_{G_i} \right) + \sum_{j=1}^{n} \left(f_{C_j}(c_{p_j}, c_{b_j}, s) + T_{Q_j}(\phi_j) \right) \tag{1}$$

for m links and n nodes.

3.6 Adaptation for real-time delivery

Subscribers always expect information being retrieved should arrive briefly after they click the service requests. But they have no idea if they have moved into regions with poor connectivities. Real-time communications are more desirable features for some mobile users, e.g., stock traders. Therefore, in this case, the content carried by the late arrivals of these packets may become unimportant. Hence, in the framework, a parameter W is known as "expected real-time constraint." A subscriber should set the W according to his or her limit of patience on waiting time in the user preference profile; if not, it can be assigned to certain default wait time in system.

Suppose there is a connection being established between a subscriber and a server. A proper path has already determined in the initial setup phase and meta-information has been exchanged. If the total round-trip delay between the client and server is T, such that the forwarding and returning delays are identical, then we have $T = 2T_D$ from Eqn. (1). The expected real-time constraint of a client should not be shorter than the round-trip delay, i.e., $W < T$; otherwise, the retrieved multimedia content can never meet the QoE of the subscriber.

In the case that $W > T$, the T_D may vary due to other traffic in networks. It may have chances to violate the real-time constraint requirement. In this scenario, the agent in the framework acts and attempts to adapt the content in order to meet the W requirement. For example, a sudden change of connecting speed, for example, from wired to wireless access link, has happened. Then content adaptation should be carried out in the network core, for example, by reducing the amount of multimedia traffic with compression and reduced frame size, in order to meet the real-time constraint. For example, the packet size has been modified, and the final delivered packet size is changed from s to s_A bytes when it reaches the subscriber.

In general, many multimedia session is composed of more than one traffic stream. In the example shown in Fig. 6, there are three traffic types in one session, and the importance of each of them is ranked. The rank 1 traffic may contain critical data of size 6,600 bytes; the rank 2 traffic may contain compressible multimedia traffic; and the rank 3 traffic carries unimportant data traffic. The ideal curve indicates that the available bandwidth changes linearly. When there is sufficient bandwidth, all traffic in this session can get the network without any adaptations, i.e., when bandwidth is larger than or equal to 50,000 bytes. But the available bandwidth starts decreasing linearly, the rank 3 data traffic should be removed, and then the rank 2 multimedia traffic should be adapted. The size reduction of the rank 2 traffic due to adaptation is not continuous. This hence leads to the staircase structure as shown. When the available bandwidth is small and then only the rank 1 critical data traffic must always be kept for delivery. This happens in this graph when s_A is below 6,600 bytes, and both the ideal and real curves should stay flat.

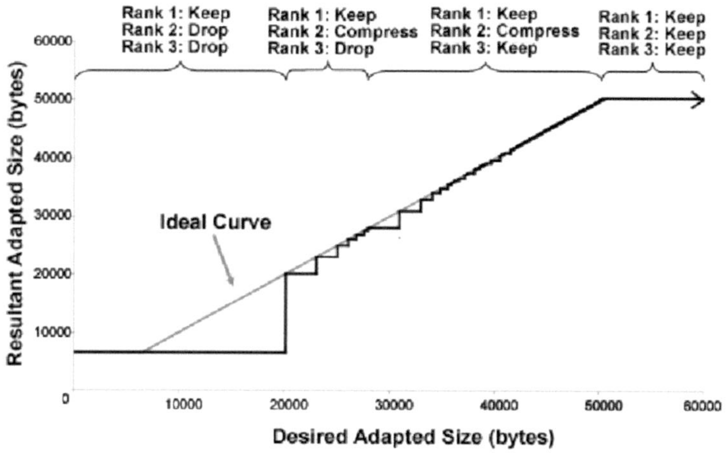

Fig. 6. Desired adapted sizes.

4. Testbed evaluation

A testbed consists of ten nodes has been set up to validate the QoS control framework for multimedia traffic. Experiments have been carried out to confirm if the proposed QoS control framework can adapt traffic content to meet the expectation of subscriber. One set of experiments is to examine the delivery of web pages with real-time information component. Another set of experiments is to adapt video stream to meet the link bandwidth constraint in real-time. For both experiments, classification of traffic types have been preset for carrying out expected component adaptation accordingly.

4.1 Real-time delivery of web pages

In this set of experiments, a web page consists of multiple informative components is sent every 2.5 seconds. As listed in Table 2, these components are pre-classified into three ranking classes based on their relative importance. Rank 1 information is considered the most important, and it should be sent to the subscriber whenever possible. Then there is a picture in the page. It belongs to rank 2 class, and can be compressed with lower resolutions upon needed. The other rank 3 components in the HTML page are for creating an appealing look of the page only. They are not as important and can be dropped if resources are running low.

During the experiments, the ingress agent computes the desired adapted size, $s_{ADAPTED}$, after learning the limiting bottleneck bandwidth through receiving the result capsules from the associated egress agent. Measured data are averaged through the last 100 samples. Certainly, wireless access link bandwidth varies due to the mobility of the user, which is simulated through changing the Linux traffic control function. Different access bandwidths are used for testings, which include 115 kbps, 1 Mbps, and 2.4 Mbps. Furthermore, we have imposed different real-time constraints for the delivery of this web page information. The patience limit of a user is interpreted as the real-time delivery constraint. For the tests, the constraints with values of 1000, 800, 600, and 400 msec are used in testbed. This limit setting indicates that the user shall re-click or reload the page when the time is reached. This is the goal of the framework to deliver at least the rank 1 traffic to the subscriber within this time constraint.

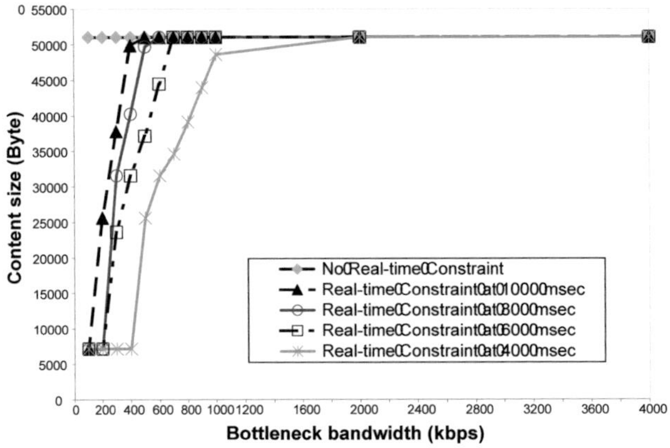

(a) Adapting sizes of web pages.

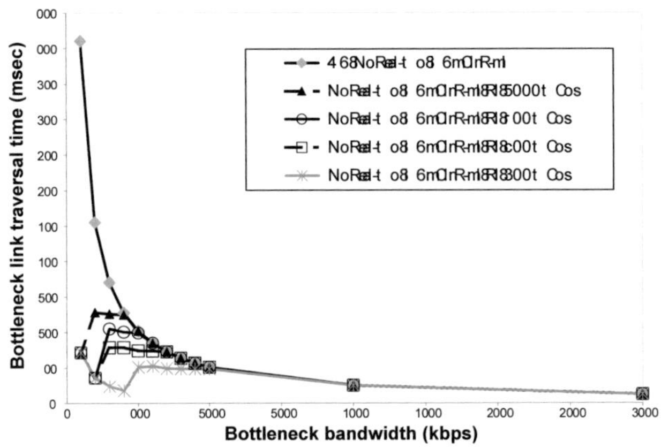

(b) Link traversal times.

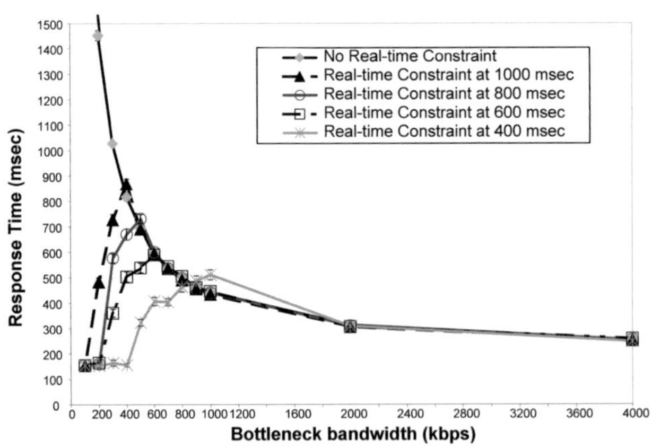

(c) Response times.

Fig. 7. Web page delivery: a) delivery size; b) traversal time; c) response time.

Rank	Content	Size (bytes)
1	real-time data	6600
2	picture	13590 - 25958
3	other data	7900

Table 2. Sizes of various components in a web page: original picture size is 25958 bytes, maximally compressed size is 13,590 bytes.

In Fig. 7(a), the measured $s_{ADAPTED}$ is shown under different user patience limits and bottleneck bandwidth. Fig. 7(b) is obtained by dividing the measured $s_{ADAPTED}$ with the bottleneck link bandwidth, thereby giving the bottleneck link traversal duration values. When selective delivery is triggered, the bottleneck link traversal time remains constant while the bandwidth is shrinking. This trend continues until only the rank 1 component is delivered. Thus, the bottleneck link traversal is the reciprocal of the bottleneck bandwidth multiplied by the size of the rank 1 component. Fig. 7(c) shows the resultant response time across the networks. If there is no limit on the patience threshold, the response time exponentially increases when the bottleneck bandwidth linearly decreases. In fact, when the bottleneck bandwidth is reduced to 100 kbps, the response time surges to $12,016 \pm 339$ msec due to the exponential increase in the backlog of data waiting to be delivered to the client at the last-mile link.

The response time characteristics under various user patience limits are similar. In general, the response time increases exponentially when the bottleneck bandwidth decreases. This trend continues until they reach their respective adaptation thresholds. From then on, the response time decreases linearly with the reduction of bandwidth. When the bandwidth decreases even further, the response time reaches a point beyond which ranks 2 and 3 in-page components are dropped. The response time stays flat at about 150 milliseconds.

4.2 Real-time delivery of images

The next set of experiments is to delivery images across networks. The bottleneck link is the access link of a subscriber. The real-time constraint W is passed from the client preference list to the server, and it can be discovered by the agents in networks. They can detect the existent of real-time constraint of a communication session, and the delivery of images based on the meta-information. If there are multiple good quality paths existing between the two agents, the ingress agent can then have multiple choices in carrying out appropriate operations inside the infrastructure. An exemplary operational details of using a single path computation in the infrastructure is shown in Fig. 8. The goal of the infrastructure is to fit the image delivery to receiver within the duration of W sec.

The image scaling operation starts when the ingress agent receives the incoming Lena BMP images, as shown in Fig. 9(a). In the experiments, the ingress agent converts them into JPEG images, forwards them along a path, and the running times are measured against the time constraints. Regularly, the egress agent reports the measured bottleneck link bandwidth to the ingress agent. Through the measurements, the image compression ratio can be estimated through operations in the infrastructure. Different scaling parameter, λ, can be set between 1 and 16 inclusively, where 16 is the best quality and 1 is the worst. The next question is to determine if the generated images with selected compression ratio can meet the real-time and bandwidth constraints. Then it leads to design of an initial calibration process. The goal of the process is to find the lowest acceptable bound of the compression ratio for a subscriber.

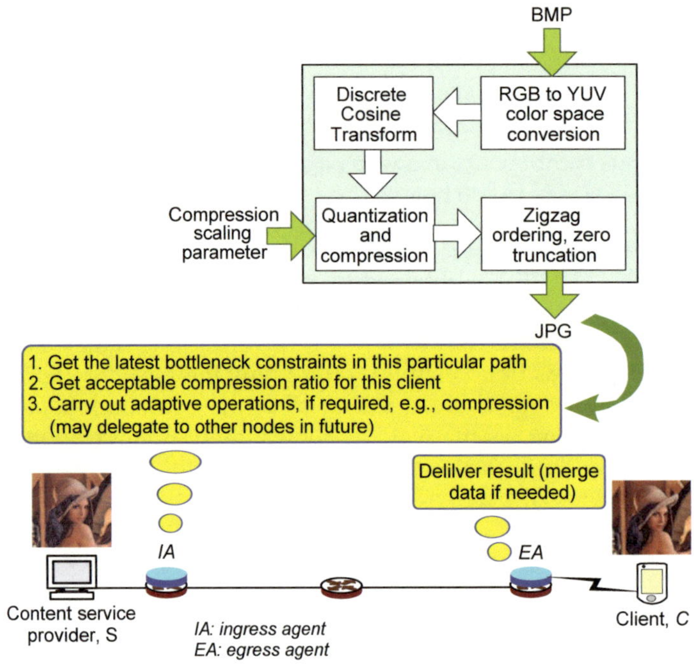

Fig. 8. Real-time image scaling operations.

λ	size (% of original)	$R_{RMS}(C,R)$	# in Fig. 9
1	24%	5.026%	(b)
2	36%	3.985%	(c)
3	45%	3.376%	(d)
4	51%	2.984%	(e)
5	55%	2.607%	(f)
6	63%	2.393%	(g)
10	77%	1.806%	(h)
13	89%	1.562%	(i)
16	100%	1.409%	(j)

Table 3. Visual quality and $R_{RMS}(C,R)$.

With different compression ratios, sizes of resulting compressed images are listed in Table 3. For example, the visual qualities of some compressed images are shown from Fig. 9(b) to Fig. 9(j). Through the initial calibration process, a subscriber can actually select the worst quality image that he or she can accept, and inform the content provider. With this information, the infrastructure can then be aware of the minimum QoE expectation of the subscriber. And from the Table, an ingress agent can pick a lowered but acceptable bounding value of the compression scaling parameter to meet the latest networking conditions, if they have just turned worse. There are two parameters that should be considered before carrying out compression operations. The first one is to determine if the real-time constraint can be met. The second is to determine if the image quality can meet the quality expectation of a user. Both conditions must be met; otherwise, the images are dropped at ingress agent, because there are no good reasons to send an unacceptable low quality images.

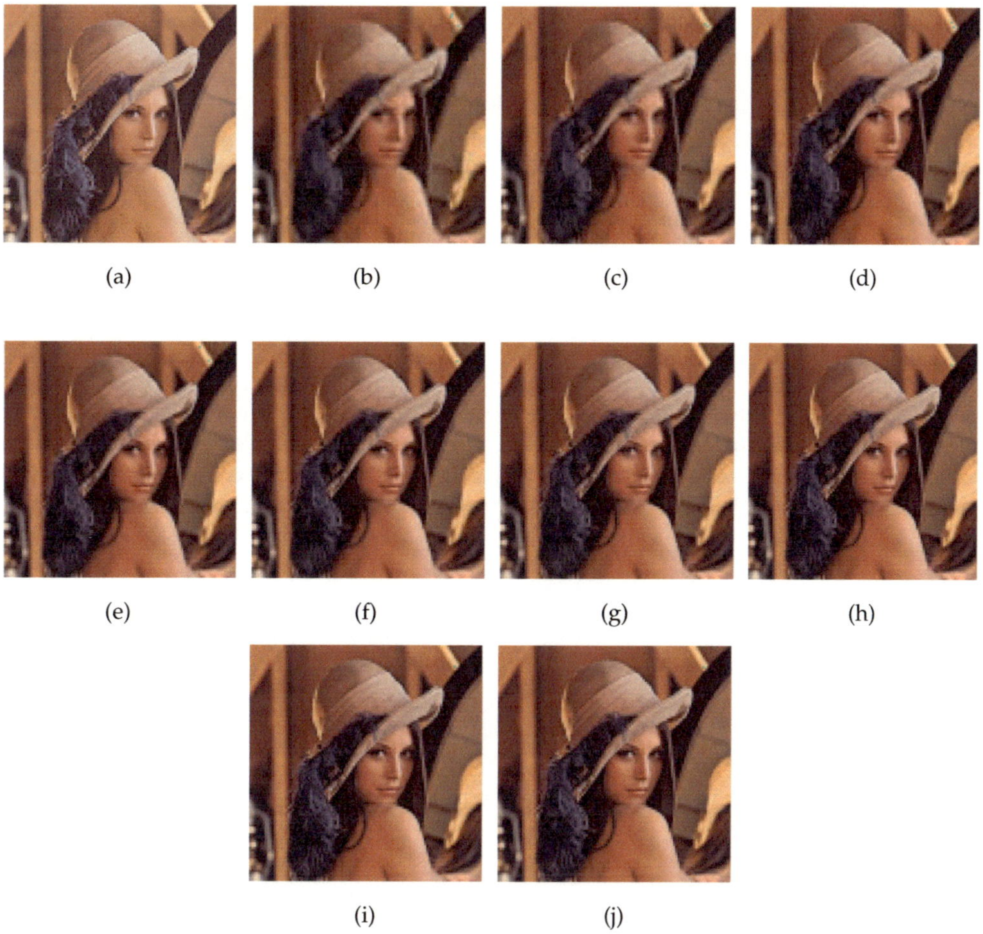

Fig. 9. Visual quality of compressed images: (a) original in bitmap format, (b)-(j) compressed in JPEG formats

4.3 Real-time delivery of streaming content

Multimedia applications, such as IPTVs, and online conference meetings, belong to the real-time streaming traffic class with temporal relationship among sending information. Typically, a streaming movie session may consist of three traffic types: video, voice, and/or data such as the subtitle. Actions are spread across multiple consecutive video frames. Apart from the blocking effects in images, video motion may not be reconstructed properly if some motion vectors for decoding are lost. As a result, subscriber could have trouble interpreting the video content. When a video is transmitted across networks, some video frames can be dropped. Then, long overdue frame group not displaying at all causes viewer waiting for long delay, and the the content may appear out-of-order. Hence, when there are more frames dropped, the reproducing video becomes jerky and gives poor perceptual interpretation.

It is important that our proposed framework can offer satisfactory experience of real-time video delivery. In the experiments, video frames are extracted from a theatrical screen advertisement promoting the 1955 Chevrolet models. The advertisement movie has long sequences of car movements. Inter-frames smoothness can be observed easily, and the perceived quality can be assessed easily.

For demonstration purpose, this movie clip does not carry voice component which is actually replaced by subtitle. Each frame in video is a 24-bit RGB bitmap image with a size of 63,414 bytes and a visual dimension of 176 × 120 pixels. The sizes of the accompanying subtitles range from 97 to 120 bytes. Compression ratio may differ frame by frame depending on the networking conditions. With the highest compression ratio, compressed frame images have sizes ranging from 8,806 bytes (13.89% of the originals) to 12,674 bytes (19.99%). Two frames are extracted every second for creating one new accompanying subtitle. Eighty-eight frames are extracted. At the server, the video clip is replayed continuously in the experiments. The relationship between compressed size and compression scaling parameter, λ, is encoded using meta-information. Thus, the network infrastructure can efficiently choose the closest adapted size, s_A, with an appropriate compression parameter λ. Then the network nodes execute compression operations according to λ. The real-time delivery scheme of the video experiment is based on a 2-level ranking levels: 1) subtitle is classified as rank 1, R_1, 2) frame image is classified as rank 2, R_2; where rank 1 has higher priority than rank 2 traffic.

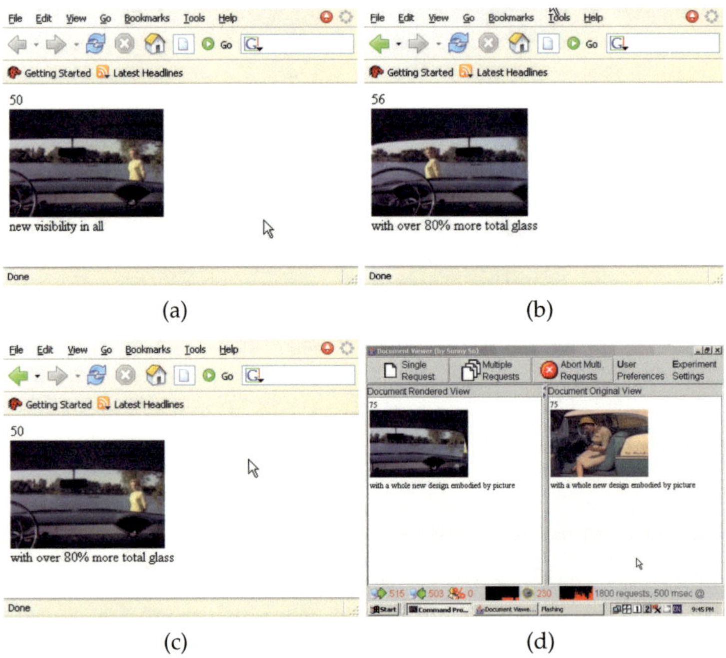

Fig. 10. (a) Frame 50, (b) frame 56, (c) time at frame 56, picture at frame 50, (d) comparing viewer with traffic load monitoring.

For video communication, the ingress agent can have choices on delivering frames across the networks. Depending on the latest measured network conditions, the agent can send frames unchanged, compressed, or simply drop the frames. Certainly, frames sent may still get dropped inside the networks due to congestion, and these are called frame lost events.

Two snapshots of the movie are shown in Fig. 10(a) and 10(b). When the network delay is too long with a real-time delay constraint being applied. Then frames are dropped at the ingress agent to reduce the traffic load in testbed. For example, as shown in Fig. 10(c), the movie is stuck at frame number 50, but the subtitle has arrived at frame 56. This implies that the proposed pervasive infrastructure can enforce certain minimal QoS quality. In this case, the receiver is still able to see the latest subtitle section, or he or she can listen to the voice part if the voice section exists. An MPEG-1 viewer at the subscriber has been created to compare a locally stored copy with the remotely retrieving video. The viewer, as shown in Fig. 10(d), also reports the packet loss and CPU consumption.

For performance measurements, the link speed of the simulated wireless access shrinks from 3 Mbps to 100 kbps. With different real-time constraints applied, different operations on video frames have been carried out. If bandwidth is abundant, frames are sent uncompressed, as in all constraint cases with link speed of 3 Mbps. But when the link rate reduces, and the real-time constraints is shorter, then more frames are compressed, or dropped. It is always important to observe that, for the cases reported in Fig. 11, the amount of frame losses inside the networks are small. This satisfies the goal of the proposed QoS control framework for multimedia traffic, that is, to deliver as much information as possible to the subscribers.

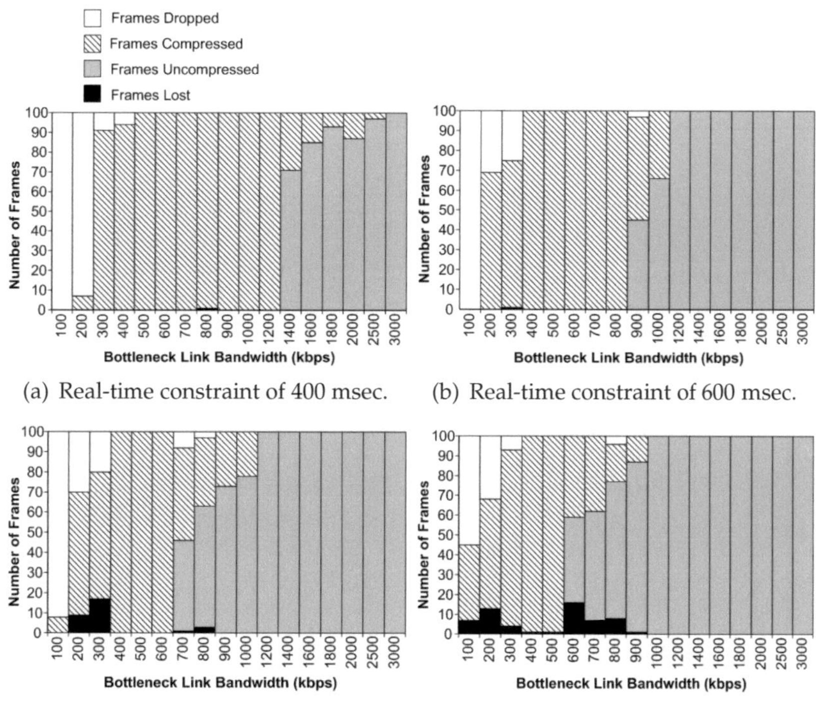

(a) Real-time constraint of 400 msec. (b) Real-time constraint of 600 msec.

(c) Real-time constraint of 800 msec. (d) Real-time constraint of 1000 msec.

Fig. 11. Video stream modifications.

5. Conclusion

In this chapter, an agent-based quality control framework for delivering satisfactory multimedia traffic across the Internet has been designed. The framework is currently built on top of existing networking protocols. The major components in the platform consists of ingress and egress agents. QoS monitoring capsules are regularly sent between agents in order to enable the ingress agent to adapt the content information, while meeting the requirements and expectations of subscribers and end-users. At the current phase, communicating protocol designs between the two agents at the edges of networks have been tested. Furthermore, different traffic types have been thoroughly experimented. Through multimedia content classification, whether it is for real-time or non-real-time, important or unimportant, traffic can be sent to subscribers to meet their expected multimedia quality in our framework. And in future, more thorough investigation shall be carried out to enable routers inside the Internet to assist and relieve the loads of the ingress and egress agents.

6. Appendix A: Visual difference predictor

One possible filter responsive function is called Visual Differences Predictor (VDP) (Daly, 1993), which can be adopted to model the retinal sensitivity of human being. The retinal response to luminance is a non-linear function, and it is used to evaluate the quality of distorted images. Algorithm derived for VDP attempts to indicate the probability of detecting a difference between the two images on a pixel-by-pixel basis. In our testing, we have adopted a simplified VDP version using a relative mean calculation. These computations may not be needed to run at all times; the image difference computations can be carried out during quality calibrations or upon user requests.

The luminous response, $l(i,j)$ shown in (2), is called amplitude non-linearity value,

$$l(i,j) = \frac{L(i,j)}{L(i,j) + c_1(L(i,j))^b} \tag{2}$$

where $L(i,j)$ is the luminance of the pixel (i,j) in dimension cd/m^2. Typically assigned values for the parameters b and c_1 are 0.63 and 12.6, respectively. Spatial frequencies $f_l(u,v)$ can be obtained through the Fast Fourier Transform of the luminance sensitivity spatial pattern $l(i,j)$. It gives the magnitude at horizontal spatial frequency at u and vertical spatial frequency at v. Human being is aware of changes in signal contrast. The contrast sensitivity function (C_S) is used to model the retinal contrast sensitivity to a spatial frequency.

$$\begin{aligned} C_S(u,v) =& (0.008\, z^{-1.5} + 1)^{-0.2} \times \\ & 1.42\sqrt{z}\, e^{-0.3\sqrt{z}} \times \sqrt{1 + 0.06 e^{0.3\sqrt{z}}} \end{aligned} \tag{3}$$

where $z = u^2 + v^2$.

The C_S, in (3), gives a two-dimensional spatial frequency plane (u,v). As shown in (4), the C_S function filters the $f_l(u,v)$ values and obtains the parameter Filtered Magnitudes of the Amplitude Non-Linearity Value (FMANLV), $g(u,v)$. The $g(u,v)$ measures the luminance sensitivity filtered by the retinal response with respect to the spatial frequency (u,v), which is

$$g(u,v) = f_l(u,v) * C_S(u,v). \tag{4}$$

A.1 Calibration operations

There are no needs to run these computations in real-time. In the proposed platform, the framework can initiate an initial calibration phase between subscriber and content provider. In other words, the ingress and egress agents can subsequently set appropriate preferences for a subscriber.

The multimedia content provider may send a reference image R with a reference $g_R(u,v)$ value. Then it sends other compressed testing image, C, with $g_C(u,v)$ at the recipient under the assumption of certain network conditions. Suppose this is the least accepted quality of a subscriber, then the egress agent can compute a relative image metric through normalizing the $g_C(u,v)$ of the test image with respect to the $g_R(u,v)$ of reference image. The resulting measure is called the relative root-mean square (RMS) error of the reference content,

$$R_{RMS}(C,R) = \sqrt{\frac{\sum_{u,v}(g_C(u,v) - g_R(u,v))^2}{\sum_{u,v} g_R(u,v)^2}} \times 100\%. \quad (5)$$

A smaller $R_{RMS}(C,R)$ value indicates that the received image is visually closer to the original one. This quality bound of a streaming multimedia content can be set through finding the largest accepted $R_{RMS}(C,R)$ value of a content subscriber. This bounding measure is returned to the ingress agent for determining appropriate compression operations in future.

7. References

Satyanarayanan M. (2001). Pervasive computing: vision and challenges. *IEEE Personal Communications*, Vol. 8, No. 4, pp. 10-17.

Winkler S. & Mohandas P. (2008). The Evolution of Video Quality Measurement: From PSNR to Hybrid Metrics, *IEEE Trans. Broadcasting*, Vol. 54, No. 3, pp. 1–8

Chen K.-T.; Tu C.-C.; Xiao W.-C. (2009). OneClick: A Framework for Measuring Network Quality of Experience, *IEEE Infocom'09*, Brazil.

Grega M.; Janowski L.; Leszczuk M.; Romaniak P.; Papir Z. (2008) Quality of Experience Evaluation for Multimedia, *Telecommunication Review*, pp. 142-158, No. 4, 2008, Poland.

Methods for Subjective Determination of Transmission Quality, Inter. Telecommunication Union (ITU-T)

Rajagopalan R. (2010). Video Quality Measurements for Mobile Networks. Openwave. http://openwave.com/sites/default/files/docs/solutions/Video Quality MeasurementsWPfinal0710.pdf

Rahrer T.; Fiandra R.; Wright S. (2006). *Triple-play Services Quality of Experience (QoE) Requirements*, DSL Forum, Architecture & Transport Working Group, Technical Report TR-126

Chen B. & Cheng H.H. (2010). A Review of the Applications of Agent Technology in Traffic and Transportation Systems, *IEEE Trans. Intelligent Transportation Systems*, Vol. 11, No. 2

Lee J.-S. & Hsu P.-L. (2007). Implementation of a Remote Hierarchical Supervision System Using Petri Nets and Agent Technology, *IEEE Trans. Systems, Man, Cybernetics - Part C*, Vol. 37, No. 1

Blake S.; Black D.; Carlson M.; Davies E.; Wang Z.; Weiss W. (1998). *An Architecture for Differentiated Services*, RFC 2475. Internet Engineering Task Force, 1998.

Law K. L. E.; Leung R. (2003). Design and Implementation of Active Network Socket Programming, *Microprocessors and Microsystems J.*, Vol. 27, Issues 5-6, pp. 277-284, June 2003.

Agarwal S.; Singh J. P.; Mavlankar A.; Bacchichet P.; Girod B. (2008). Performance of P2P Live Video Streaming Systems on a Controlled Test-bed, *Tridentcom'08*, Mar. 18-20, 2008, Innsbruck, Austria.

Huang Y.; Fu T. Z. J.; Chiu D.-M.; Lui J. C. S.; Huang C. (2008). Challenges, Design and Analysis of a Large-scale P2P-VoD System, *ACM Sigcomm'08*, Aug. 17-22, 2008, Seattle, USA.

Jrad Z. E.-F.; Benmammar B.; Correa J.; Krief F.; Mbarek N. (2005). A User Assistant for QoS Negotiation in a Dynamic Environment Using Agent Technology, *2nd IFIP Inter. Conf. Wireless Optical Communications Networks (WOCN)*, pp. 270-274

Pratistha I. M.; Zaslavsky A.; Cuce S.; Dick M. (2005). Improving Operational Efficiency of Web Services with Mobile Agent Technology, *IEEE/WIC/ACM Inter. Conf. Intelligent Agent Technology*, pp. 725-731

Banavar G. & Bernstein A. (2002). Software infrastructure and design challenges for ubiquitous computing, *Communications of the ACM*, Vol. 45, No. 12, pp. 92-96

Noble B. D. (2000). System support for mobile, adaptive applications, *IEEE Personal Communications*, pp. 44-49

Lum W. Y. & Lau F. C. M. (2002). A context-aware decision engine for content adaptation," *IEEE Pervasive Computing*, pp. 41-49

Byers J. W.; Considine J.; Mitzenmacher M.; Rost S. (2004). Informed Content Delivery Across Adaptive Overlay Networks, *IEEE/ACM Trans Networking*, Vol. 12, No. 5

Perkins C. (2002). *IP Mobility Support for IPv4*, IETF, RFC 3344

Johnson D.; Perkins C.; Arkko J. (2004). *IP Mobility Support for IPv6*, IETF, RFC 3775

Law K. L. E. & Lau C. (2010). Mobility Service Agent, *3rd IEEE Workshop on Wireless and Internet Services (WISe)*, in conjunction with *35th IEEE Conference on Local Computer Networks (LCN)*

Daly S. (1993). The Visible Differences Predictor: an Algorithm for the Assessment of Image Fidelity, *Digital Images and Human Vision*, Editor: A.B. Watson, pp.179-206, MIT Press, Cambridge MA

Stoica T.; Morris R.; Karger D.; Kaashoek F.; Balakrishnan H. (2001). Chord: A scalable Peer-To-Peer lookup service for internet applications, *ACM SIGCOMM'01*, Aug. 2001.

Part 2

Social Networking Using Multimedia

3

Mobile Application GPS-Based

Berta Buttarazzi
University of "Tor Vergata", Rome, Italy

1. Introduction

Most of navigators for mobile devices have a big failure; they do not notify the user of road condition (traffic, checkpoints, car accidents, road work) unless the user has some kind of paid subscription. Even in this case the only information that are provided are about traffic. Many famous Navigators notify user of traffic using sensors under the road, but it is not a real time update. Besides there is virtually no way to notify user of car accidents or checkpoints at real time, user usually downloads POIs (Points of Interest) from Internet and uploads them to the Navigator which will display them on the map.

Road condition change very frequently so POIs should be updated faster so that an user can decide to take another road to avoid traffic, to reduce pollution, to save time. An humble application like this can also be used in a very useful way to get our life better!

The purpose of this work has been to study and develop a way that displays updated POIs on a map. Thanks to the Web 2.0 philosophy the best way that has been found is to allow users to report any events on the road. Users can also report if an event no longer exists so that markers on the map can be updated in the fastest and most accurate way possible. Because of high interaction between users, this application is like a Social Network where the relationship between users are based on GPS positions.

Mobile devices are obviously the best devices to do that, thanks to their integrated GPS sensor and to the easy development environment like Android SDK. Android has been chosen because it is completely open source and because it is a Google OS and it can be used in the best way in conjunction with Google Maps.

2. Environment

2.1 MOBILE WEB 2.0

World Wide Web was born in 1993 and in the latest 20 years there is a completely new way of using it. After Web 2.0 philosophy has developed since 1999, new technologies and new ways of approaching the Internet were born.

In Web 1.0 Users could only access website to retrieve information. These information were written by the webmaster and read by the users. Web 2.0 introduced a fast change of approach. Contents were created not only by webmasters, but also by the users. Broadband connection helped a lot users to connect to the Internet and to publish their contents.

Websites like Wikipedia, YouTube and Flickr had a large impact on World Wide Web. developments of Web 2.0.

We can say that the biggest differences between Web 1.0 and Web 2.0 are the following:

- Web 1.0 was about reading, while Web 2.0 is about writing;
- Web 1.0 was about client-server, while Web 2.0 is about peer to peer;
- Web 1.0 was about wires, while Web 2.0 is about wireless;
- Web 1.0 was about home pages, while Web 2.0 is about blogs;
- Web 1.0 was about web forms, while Web 2.0 is about web applications;
- And many others…

Users started to share their thoughts, their ideas and their multimedia content on these websites and they start to interact between each other more and more. In 1997 this interaction had a blast when Social Network like Facebook started to have a lot of users.

A Social Network is a social structure made up of individuals which are connected by one or more interdependency, like friendship in Facebook. It is important to notice how much Social Network are used nowadays.

Between the end of 2007 and the beginning of 2008 mobile devices with Apple OS and Android OS entered the market. A new kind of Web was born; everything that could be done in our home in front of a PC could be done everywhere by using a smartphone. Besides new technologies created new ways to use the Internet. GPS Sensor embedded in the smartphone could help locate the user's position so navigation via satellite could be done by simple smartphones instead of ad hoc navigator (like TomTom).

In 2011 smartphones sales beat PC sales for the first time in history. It is an important change, we are not talking about Web 2.0, but we are in the Mobile Web 2.0 era.

2.2 Android

Android is an operating system for mobile devices such as smartphones and tablet. It consists in a Kernel based on Linux Kernel, with middleware, libraries and APIs written in C and application software running on application framework which includes Java compatible libraries. Uses the Dalvik Virtual Machine to run compiled Java Code.

Current version is now the 3.2 Honeycomb released in July,2011, which is an incremental release that adds new capabilities like zoom-to-fill screen compatibility mode; capability to load media files directly from the SD card.

It uses SQLite to store datas, OpenGL ES 2.0 for 3d Graphics. It includes GPS Sensor, Accelerometer, Gyroscope, Magnetomer, Proximity and Pressure Sensor, Thermometers. Supports multi-touch and Bluetooth and is multitasking.

It provides an Eclipse Tool inside the SDK to help developer program in Eclipse Environment.

3. Application

The application is divided into 2 smaller applications:

1. Android Application: it is on the mobile device and it displays current information on Google Maps, allows user to report any events by tapping the map, updates Social Network status.
2. Server Application: it communicates with the DB where all the information about users and events are stored. Android Application and Server Application communicate between them with a SSL connection.

3.1 Android application

It is the biggest and most important part of the entire application. It uses Android SDK API to manage the GPS Sensor, Google Maps API to show the Map powered by Google Maps, to display the markers about events on the Map. The other classes must send information to the Server or to Facebook/Twitter App.

The first and most important part is acquiring the User's Location. It's important to manage it properly because the aim is to get the most accurate location and use the least battery possible.

Android utilizes GPS and Android's Network Location Provider to acquire the user location. Although GPS is most accurate, it only works outdoors, it quickly consumes battery power, and doesn't return the location as quickly as users want. Android's Network Location Provider determines user location using cell tower and Wi-Fi signals, providing location information in a way that works indoors and outdoors, responds faster, and uses less battery power.

Obtaining user location from a mobile device can contain errors and be inaccurate due to:

- Multitude of location sources: determining which to use and trust between GPS, Cell-ID, and Wi-Fi;
- User movement: location changes and we need to re-estimating user location every so often;
- Varying accuracy: a location obtained 10 seconds ago from one source might be more accurate than the newest location from another or same source.

Android provides a best performance model to obtain user location:

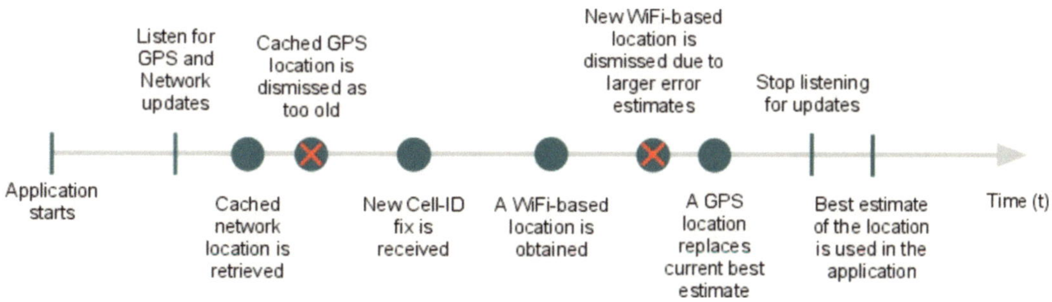

Fig. 1. Timeline representing the window in which an application listens for location updates

The application will start listen to location updates just after it started. After a certain amount of time the application will come back to listen to updates and will estimate the best location between the old one and the one just retrieved.

The best way to get the most accurate location is to use the API method *getAccuracy()*. This method returns the accuracy of the fix in meters. If for example this method returns an *Accuracy* value of 50, it means that user is in a 50 meters radius from the position that is shown on the map.

However if we want a location to be the most accurate possible, we have to use a lot of battery, so we should save some of our battery and have a less accurate location.

There are several tricks we can use to save device battery which is fundamental in this application:

1. Reduce the size of the window above in which we listen to location updates, less time the GPS sensor will be on the less battery will be used;
2. Using a last known location to increase the speed the location is shown on the map (every first time the application is launched, it takes a while to get a fix of the current location, because the GPS sensor must connect to several satellites);
3. Requesting location updates less frequently;
4. Use just one of the two providers (GPS and Network).

Obviously these tricks have a con: they don't help us to get a very accurate location. But the objective is to have the application works for a long time.

To achieve the most valuable result this application uses the following algorithm to save device's battery:

1. Check if the retrieved location is more recent than the one we are using by *getTime()*;
2. Check if the retrieved location has a better Accuracy than the one we are using by *getAccuracy()*;
3. Check which provider is more dependable and use a location retrieved by that provider.

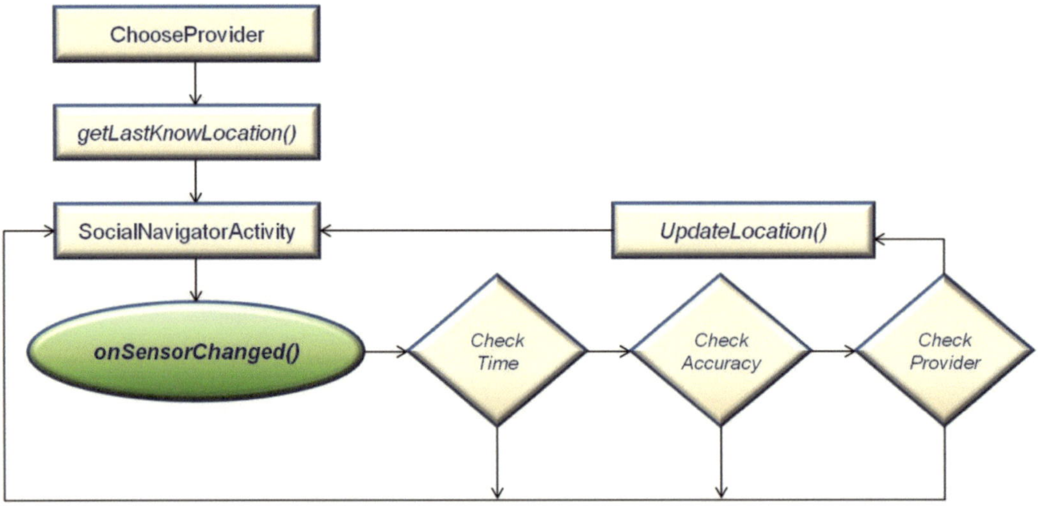

Fig. 2. Algorithm to choose the best location saving battery.

The problem is when the GPS sensor is off or when there is no GPS signal (i.e. when we are in buildings). The Android Network Provider will first get the Cell ID and then will send it to google server, which maps such Cell IDs and the server will return a latitude and longitude. In this case accuracy is usually very low, for example 1000 meters. By this time Android will also try to see all WiFi networks in the area and will send information about them too to the google server and if possible google server will return a new location with higher accuracy for an example 800 meters. It is very important to notice that the Network Provider requires an internet connection. So if the user is in a building and there is no data connection, he will never be able to get a location.

Once the application has the user's location, it will connect to the server and download the list of events and their location and it will show a map centered in the user's location and will display the markers of the events that are around him, as shown in the next figure.

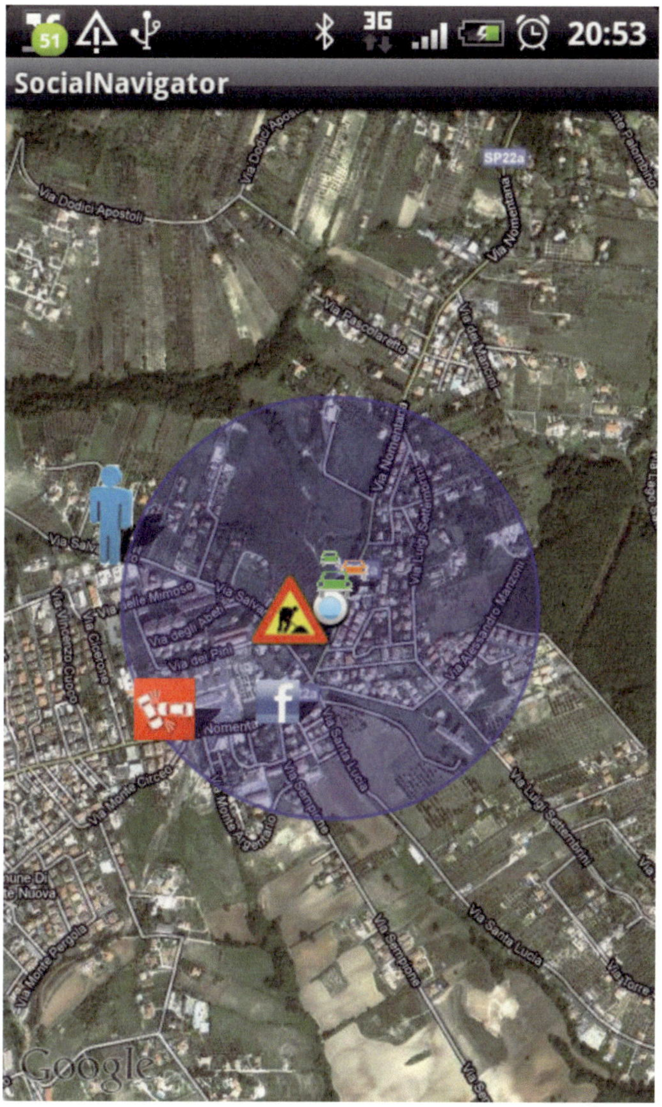

Fig. 3. View of the Map on the Mobile Device with the markers of traffic, road works, car accidents, FB events and friends

In the above figure we can see different markers:

- Our position in the center;
- One of our friends;
- A car accident;
- Traffic jam;
- Road Work;
- A Facebook event.

The user can tap on any of these events to see more information or delete them if he realizes that the reported event is no more in that location.

Fig. 4. Info Dialog about an event (in this case an accident).

Events like car accidents will be automatically deleted by the server after 24 hours after they have been reported.

If an user wants to report a new event, he can tap twice on the map and the application will ask him what kind of event he is reporting. After that the application will compose a message and send an update request to the server.

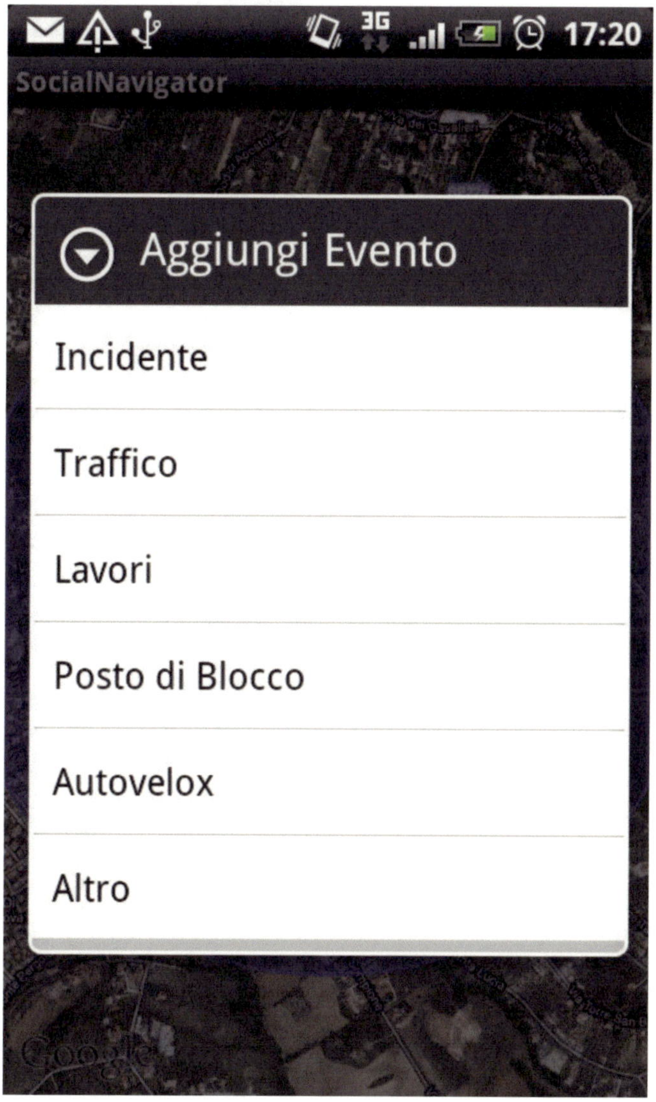

Fig. 5. Dialog to report a new event.

The application can show position of user's friends (after downloading the friend list from Facebook). The information that an user can see by tapping on a people marker are name and phone number and he can decide to call or text his friend from inside the app. The application will also notify the user if any of his friends is close to him so that he can call them.

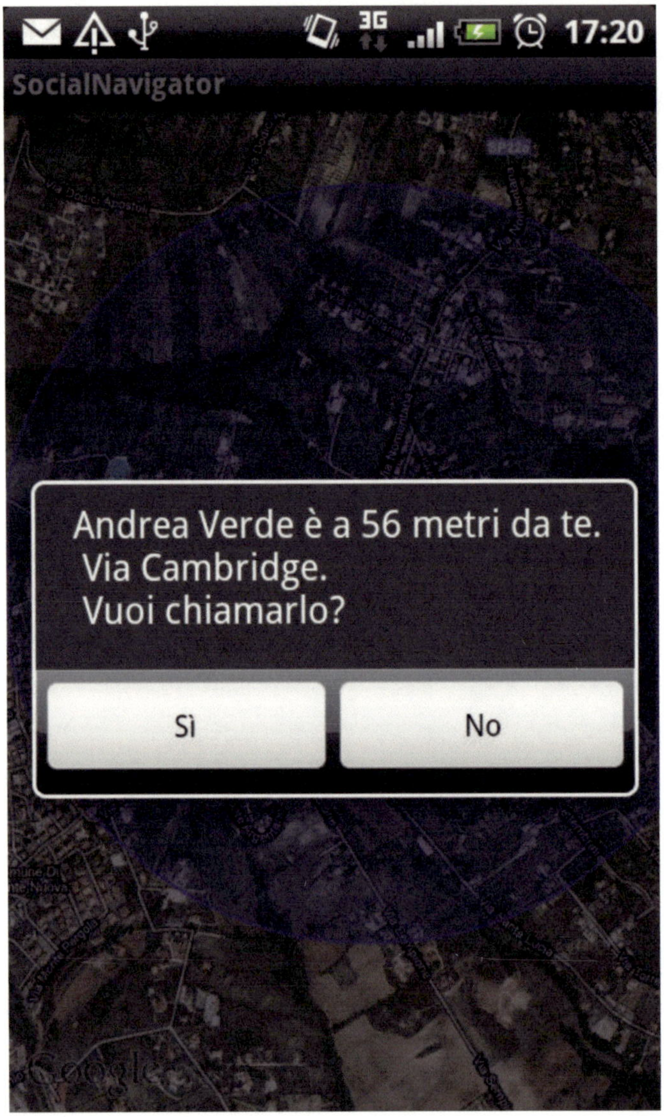

Fig. 6. Dialog that report a friend's position near to us

It is also important to give the user the chance to manage his privacy, so he can decide which markers he wants to see and he can decide if he wants his friends to see his location on their Map. Besides he can also decides if he wants to share his reports on Social Network like Facebook and Twitter.

Thanks to Android API, it is possible to check the speed an user is moving using the GPS Sensor so the application can understand by itself if there is traffic on the road. Obviously there is the chance that the user has momentarily stopped and there is not traffic, so if the speed decreases for a certain time under 15 km/h the application will ask the user if he is in a traffic jam. In case of a positive answer (user will see a dialog and will just have to click a YES or NO button) the application will update the server with the location of a traffic jam.

Fig. 7. Privacy Preferences

One of the big problem is that the original MapView doesn't allow the user to add anything on it, but it only handles zoom in/out. The idea was to handle three different types of interaction between user and screen:

1. One single tap on a marker that opens a dialog with information about the event
2. Two taps on the map to open a dialog from which user can choose what kind of event report
3. Zoom in/out in the same way of all the other smartphones, using two fingers.

Login into the applications is very simple, Android stores user's Google credentials and the application uses them to retrieve user info, like name and friends.

3.2 Server application

This application must communicate with the application on the mobile device. It will receive data about new or old (if they have to be removed) events and it will update the DB. Every type of event has its own table in the DB, and every record has latitude, longitude, date/time and id of the user that has reported it. The People Table is a little more articulate because it has also the Facebook friend list and all the permissions the user has granted.

The events that the server application must handle are:

- Mobile device notifies user's data to the server;
- Mobile device notifies its location to the server;
- Mobile device requests to retrieve events' list;
- Mobile device requests to update events' information.

4. Conclusion

This application overcomes many limitations of Navigator and Social Network. It can be seen as a point of union between a Navigator and a Social Network. It proves the use of GPS not only for user's advantages but for more people because reports about road condition can be seen also by people that don't use the application but have access to user's Facebook/Twitter profile.

It helps users to avoid traffic and to choose another road so it can be useful not only to reduce traffic but also to reduce pollution and to protect environment.

Its strength and at the same time limitation is the fact that it is a mobile application. So it can completely use the GPS but that means it will use a lot of battery. If battery duration will increase, this kind of application could be on every mobile device and a lot of other markers could be added.

In future there can be a lot of good developments, for example it can be useful use vocal commands to report events. It could also be implemented VOIP and data connection between users. The limitation of these future developments is in the lack of APIs by Android and programs for VOIP like Skype.

5. References

Book

Reto Meier, 2010, *Professional Android 2 Application Development.* Wiley Publishing Inc., Indianapolis, USA

M. Carli, 2011,*Android 3 Guida per lo sviluppatore,* Apogeo, Italy

Endarnoto, Pradipta, Nugroho, Purnama,2011, *Traffic Condition Information Extraction & Visualization from Social Media Twitter for Android Mobile Application ,* International Conference on Electrical Engineering and Informatics, 17-19 July 2011, Bandung, Indonesia

Russello, Crispo, Fernandes, Zhauniarovich, *2011, YAASE: Yet Another Android Security Extension,* IEEE SocialCom 2011 & PASSAT 2011, October 9-11, 2011, MIT, Boston, USA

D.Rosenblum, 2007, *What Anyone Can Know: The Privacy Risks of Social Networking Sites,* Security & Privacy, IEEE, May-June 2007, Volume: 5 Issue:3- pages: 40 - 49

Website

http://developer.android.com/index.html

4

Social Networking and Science Research: The MIT-UPV and Metal 2.0 Cases

Gil Pechuán Ignacio, Conesa Garcia M. Pilar and Peris Ortiz Marta
Business Management Department,
Technical University of Valencia, Valencia,
Spain

"Social connections are one of our hallmarks. It has often been considered that these connections are what distinguish us from animals or the lack of civilization." N.A. Christakis, J. H. Fowler

1. Introduction

The value of social networking for business isn't so clear but in other areas it has been very advanced, as in the world of collaborative research and business at the international level, can affect joint enterprise (enterprise-level) is displayed as shown in the results of the collaboration project Networking between MIT and the UPV (http://mitupv.mit.edu) and UPV and AIMME[1] (http://www.metal20.org/).

Most of the measurable benefits such as improved collaboration and multimedia documentation are already in place. In terms of all the components of social networking, being on a single platform, we already have that, too, in the form of unified communications (UC).

2. "MIT-UPV exchange"

This experience is a Web-based co-operative learning project between the Massachusetts Institute of Technology (MIT) in the USA and the Universidad Politécnica de Valencia (UPV) in Spain which has been underway since 2000. Its aim is to put in contact technological students in Valencia (Spain) and technological students in Boston (USA) by means of a jointly developed interactive website. This website is an open platform that allows the registered students to interact with each other; building a technological social networking not only by using text-based messages (including a built-in chat facility), but also by uploading and downloading multimedia files, i.e. videos and graphics created by the students themselves. The contents of the website are updated in real time and are fully developed and controlled by the participating students themselves, so as to reflect their interests, views and other cultural and social components.

---

[1] Metallurgical technology institute http://www.aimme.es

2.1 Project's rationale

The Internet, in general, and the World Wide Web, in particular, represent an emerging medium for teaching, and their significant potential for the teaching/learning in a collaborative format. In order to put the impact of Web 2.0 in general and particularly the social networking into perspective from a future societal standpoint (for the students), it must first be seen from the context of how the next generation of services that are available online, specifically designed for ensuring a high degree of collaboration, information sharing, and support for knowledge-based.

Such projects are aligned with the demands of what Manuel Castells called network society.

The living environment that we have outside the classroom, in a visual world that is increasingly more technologized, makes the number of inputs of information and knowledge received outside the classroom far exceeds the amount received in them. Such a large amount of knowledge and information our students do not receive in an organized manner, in contrast to received wisdom within their educational time sequences where the transmission of knowledge is much more organized and regulated. Nowadays, it is a reality that media communication and human relations at a distance and through the network are a universal phenomenon in almost all over the world to a greater or lesser extent. This fact and the circumstances have to be assumed by the educational process and its human components-mostly the teacher-establishment because in any case countereducation - or reeducation-producing life and social environment in which they grow technologized youth is a force that competes with the transmission of knowledge organized and sequenced regulated processes of education. To enable that countereducation doesn't interfere and, worse, be set against the teaching process. They must take and integrate social instruments that are already being used by young people. Audiovisual communication, multimedia and new possibilities and constraints of the "network society" should be incorporated into the educational track that leads to evolutionary changes in the methodology of education, teaching and learning for both teachers and for students, because as we have seen in this project interactions with new media; new methods and new situations arise causing unforeseen possibilities and unexpected opportunities while students also learn to overcome difficulties.

The Web constitutes an innovative format for content delivery and information exchange. That is one reason why knowledge and use of the Web would justify its inclusion within the curriculum of a university that focuses on technology. "In addition, there are many skills where our students will be developed, adapted, extended or even reinvented in the use of technology as a professional key development through collaborative processes" as future company managers.

2.2 Defining the concept of web 2.0

Taken together, these applications form the collaboration platform that social networking applications and their variations, including mash-ups and blogs, rely on in order to accomplish high levels of collaboration. In keeping with unbounded systems thinking, the proliferation of the series of Web 2.0 applications and their growth are defined more by communication patterns than adherence to taxonomies and architectures. This is one of the factors that were taken into account in defining unbounded systems thinking as the method of enquiry.

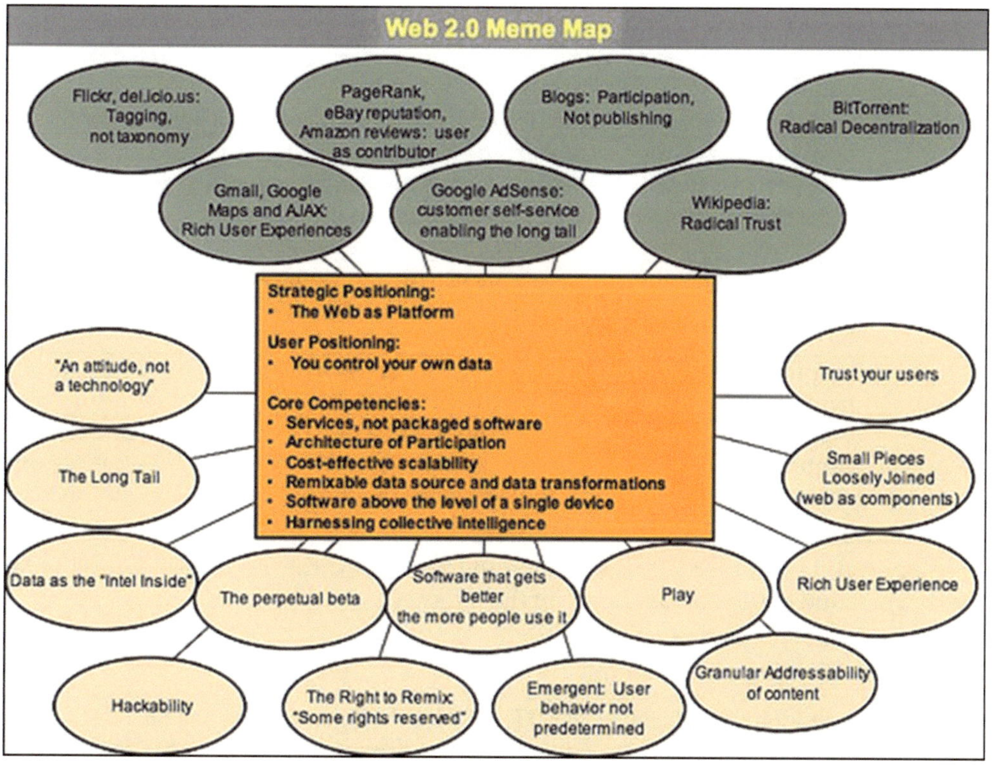

Fig. 1. The map that O'Reilly and Battelle created to show how both market and user dynamics are defining social networking (O'Reilly, 2005. et.al.).

In order to teach these skills, the pedagogical bases that lay the foundations for the use of the WWW within this project are:

- Communicative Language Teaching (and learning). Students are collaborating in a foreign language in a natural and spontaneous way, so language use is promoted by theirs mere use.
- Learner-centred pedagogy. The students themselves choose topics for interaction, as well its pace and format, according to their personal interests.
- Learning autonomy. The students are co-managers of their own learning process, and therefore take full responsibility for the related training contents, instead of merely digesting information in a passive manner.
- Learning by doing (experiential learning). In order to be able to participate, students must learn -in a practical way- how to get in the new medium and environment of Internet and multimedia formats (image processing, audio and video, etc.).
- Collaborative learning. Students find themselves totally integrated in a virtual learning and exchange community. Interaction with peers is a basic requirement to advance in the learning process.
- Cultural exchange. Students experience first-hand direct contact with the cultural systems, values and environment of their partners on the other side of the world.

Table 1 provides an overview of Web 2.0 applications, illustrating the role of social networking in the next generation of services available on the Internet.

Application	Description
Blog	Self-managed personal Web site which is made up of individual entrances and they are organized by inverse chronology
Wiki	Web site where any user qualified by the system can easily edit a content
Mash-up	Formed hybrid applications from existing applications.
Social networking	Applications in which any user is able to contact with other users generating a portfolio of contacts that is manageable. Its business use is the possibility of being able to identify experts in a concrete subject
Podcast	Entrances of multimedia contents of video or audio lodged in applications type blog. The distribution is similar to each blog post. Its proliferation may be due to RSS syndication.
Social tagging	Applications that allow classify digital contents by tags, assigned by the user, being able to share them with other users of the network.
Syndication RSS	It allows the users syndicated to a Web site to be warned of the updates content without the necessity of going to the Website. It implies the use of a content tag software (like googlereader, bloglines…) that manages the syndications of the Websites as wished by the user

Table 1. An overview of Web 2.0 applications, illustrating the role of social networking in the next generation of services available on the Internet.

2.3 Web 2.0 in learning and teaching

Samples of areas and approaches where MIT-UPV has had good effect has been:
Group work can often be aided by having social software available - this is no surprise when we note that social software is software that facilitates group process. Thus, for example: blogs can be used in personal writing and the group gives its opinion.

Social constructivism (Vygotsky , 1978) has, as a central precept, that knowledge is created by learners in the context of and as a result of social interaction. Social constructivist approaches are particularly aided by MIT-UPV as mediating mechanisms between collaborating students and between students and teachers, particularly between students who might sometimes be working in different places and at different times. Thus, for example, a group of students might construct a device in a wiki, but also be guided by a teacher who provides the fundamentals in the same wiki.

Constructionism, advocated by Seymour Papert, is particularly amenable to Web 2.0 approaches. In Papert's words 'Constructionism … shares constructivism's connotation of learning as "building knowledge structures" irrespective of the circumstances of the learning. It then adds the idea that this happens felicitously especially in a context where the learner is consciously engaged in constructing a public entity, whether it is a sandcastle on the beach or a theory of the universe" (Papert, 1991). Thus social software systems can be used for the construction of public entities, for example, via a video presentation on a social media system, a blog entry (for individual work) and a set of wiki pages (for individual and group work).

2.4 Changes in student population

Web 2.0 technologies are one of several digital technologies that are increasingly helping change some characteristics of current and future students, and these changes may necessitate profound changes in learning and teaching methods.

Marc Prensky (1978) defined 'digital natives' as a generation that has grown up with digital technology, operating at "twitch speed", and performing multiple activities simultaneously. Thus Oblinger and Oblinger characterize the next generation ("n-gen") students as digitally literate, highly Internet familiar, connected via networkedmedia, used to immediate responses, preferring experiential learning, highly social ("being a friend of a friend is acceptable"), prefer to work in teams, craving interactivity in image rich environments (as opposed to text intensive environments), and having a preference "for structure rather than ambiguity". Oblinger and Oblinger also point to a different kind of student, one who is non-traditional and working and studying at the same time.

Questions arise: Are these new student skill and preference sets different enough to demand changes in teaching methods to successfully engage with them? Do the skill sets of incoming students demand (possibly only transitional) 'remedial' teaching, for example, in using libraries and finding primary sources? Is the changing student profile going to need different ways of teaching that, e.g., minimise traditional patterns of attendance and increase flexibility in where and when learning takes place? Somewhat anecdotally, there are different perspectives relating to student engagement (and therefore grades and retention):

- We have seen reports of lecturers moving part or all of their electronic course support from traditional virtual learning environments to social networking systems like MySpace and Facebook, because of greater student engagement with these kinds of social networking tool. Web 2.0 enabled approaches may therefore help engage with students. However, there is also evidence that many students see these as "their" space that should not be 'invaded' by faculty (Hewitt, 2006).
- On the other hand, recent student interviews in a UK university revealed that students were not concerned how they are taught (e.g. through lectures, seminars, or through a blended learning approach) as long as the instruction was good. This then raises the question of what is good practice in learning and teaching in different modalities.

The emergence of a computational social science shares with other nascent interdisciplinary fields (e.g., sustainability science) the need to develop a paradigm for training new scholars. A key requirement for the emergence of an interdisciplinary area of study is the development of complementary and synergistic explanations spanning different fields and scales. Tenure committees and editorial boards need to understand and reward the effort to publish across disciplines. Certainly, in the short run, computational social science needs to be the work of teams of social and computer scientists. In the long run, the question will be: should the academic world train computational social scientists, or teams of computationally literate social scientists and socially literate computer scientists?

The emergence of cognitive science in the 1960s and 1970s offers a powerful model for the development of a computational social science. Cognitive science emerged out of the power of the computational metaphor of the human mind. It has involved fields ranging from neurobiology to philosophy to computer science. It attracted the investment of substantial resources to establish a common field, and it has created enormous progress for public good in the last generation. We would argue that a computational social science has a similar potential, and is worthy of similar investments.[2]

[2] Life in the network: the coming age of computational social science.

2.5 Possible issues and problems

An incomplete set of additional problems and issues that arise in relation to MIT-UPV are:

1. Many students work is about content sharing and repurposing. This can easily be seen by students as part of a new teenage copy-and-paste culture that runs counter to traditional notions of plagiarism, and adjustments may need to be made, either to redefine plagiarism (unlikely to occur), or to help students transcend this culture in the environments (more likely to occur).
2. There may be changes in teacher roles like the emphasis on active learning, with creation, communication and participation playing key roles, and on changing roles for the teacher, indeed, even a collapse of the distinction between teacher and student altogether.
3. There may be skills and/or culture crisis as traditional teachers are forced to use unfamiliar tools and work in unfamiliar ways and alien environments.
4. There may be economic factors at work, particularly in a world of broad participation. Not all students may be digitally connected (with a computer and Internet connection) at home or in their halls. These students would be at a profound disadvantage in a new teaching/learning concept world.

The MIT-UPV project was selected in 2010 by publisher Ian Lancashire through its publication Language Learning and technology[3], as one of the 20 world's most prestigious on-line projects.

2.6 Conclusions

The project has two complementary facets, namely, the academic exchange at all levels, and the development of an ideal university model from and for the students. Both of these aspects could evolve in the near future in an independent, yet complementary, way. It is also feasible, as has already been suggested earlier, to work co-operatively towards a deeper understanding of both university systems, and even to take a step ahead towards a university system which better meets the needs and expectations of our students. All this is closely related to total quality management and improvement; a goal for both institutions.

MIT-UPV Exchange provides a nearly-ideal meeting point between teaching innovation and the improvement of global quality within our university systems. Regarding the former aspect (teaching and learning), the project has emerged as a contextualized application of core Internet technology and the World Wide Web to learning and training, both in technical and in international collaborative skills. Concerning the second component (quality), the experience is a powerful tool to assess specific needs, suggestions and problems within the university, always from the point of view of its main clients, the students.

The flexibility of the project makes it even possible to go one step ahead of web-based exchanges and achieve a more direct and personal link between human beings (not only via computers) in both universities.

3. Metal 2.0 research project: Presentation

The METAL 2.0 project is a project of collective learning, which lasted for four years; initiated in 2008, where it has been tried to evaluate each one of the 2.0 Web tools and its

[3] Teaching Literature and Language Online. Ian Lancashire (Ed.) http://www. allbusiness. com/education-training/education-systems-institutions/15946766-1. html # ixzz1d6z72PRu

possible implantation in companies at individual and/or collective level from the accumulated experience managing the infometal marketplace (www.infometal.com) which has conceived for 6 years as one of the first enterprise social networks of the country.

The project is carried out in cooperation between Metal-Processing Technology Institute (AIMME) and the EBIM (Electronic Business Information Management) Group of investigation of the Polytechnic University of Valencia.

Unlike personal social networks (the users register then add their friends or relatives for fun), or professional social networks (the users register, then they add their professional contacts related to purchases/sales, cooperation, etc.), in enterprise social networks, the users are the enterprise associations and they register their associates, and these associates anonymously use the network for purchases/sales, finding out the positions of other companies or extracting data that they may wish to use).

3.1 Uses of Web 2.0 in metal 2.0 project

Phase 1: 2008/2009
The EBIM group has identified three phases in the use of Web 2.0. These phases are: the participation of the user, the generation of conversations in the digital environment and the collaborative work. The passage from one stage to another depends on several factors which they emphasize: the culture of use of 2.0 Web and later the degree of relation of the users in the use that is being carried out (it is not the same to work in a common project as to answer a post in a personal blog). The project METAL 2.0 is located within first stage of use of Web 2.0. Within this one it emphasizes with the result of hearing generation. Concretely the potential of relation of Web 2.0 is being operated. Generating a win all environments by taking advantage of the visibility that offers the digital surroundings and the facility to establish relations through content can be gotten to establish work contracts since Internet is talking back every better time the way in than the people we interacted.

3.2 Action, diffusion and results

After the day of presentation of the Project 'METAL 2.0: Social networks and Web 2.0 for business enterprises, which was attended by a total of 60 companies; published the videos of the same one in Internet with the purpose of forming free to the user companies of these technologies, and asking for their support in the completion of the survey of the project.

These videos have been an awareness and a woken up of these companies with respect to innovation. A 17,324 downloads in the first 5 months, visitors are from 44 countries, 38 universities, business schools and research centers. Data exceeded all expectations.
After the publication in Internet, the survey got more than 200 answers.

The initiative EXPERIMENT METAL 2.0, with 573 participating companies to date, aims at encouraging ICT´s professionals of the companies that still do not use Web 2.0 to find out about these technologies and their environments, to train purchasing and sales manager, so that they begin to experience the use of social networks and make profitable use of its power to obtain many contacts. This way, it would be possible to use their own social networks to spread the ICT and to become familiar with these tools.

As far as the diffusion of the present results of the project, there are 141 references to it: http://www.metal20.org/difusion/

As far as collaborators in the diffusion they appear a total of 36 companies and organizations, with CENATIC and CEV as new features. We remind you that any organization and/or company interested in helping in the diffusion can do it free by following the steps indicated in: http://www.metal20.org/colaboradores/

Phase 2: 2010/2011 (Metal Project Crowdsourcing 2.0)
Conclusions of the Report:
Crowdsourcing as a concept is not totally new. It's a word that brings together a considerable number of initiatives that existed long ago, even before the adoption of the term. However, its adoption has significantly facilitated to identify their common features, which have allowed us to study and propose its basic features, critical success factors, failure and environments where its use is advisable.

From the scientific point of view, crowdsourcing can be a dynamic process within companies. By using the collective intelligence of knowledge as a heterogeneous set of users, you can get novel solutions to various business problems, whether new or constantly occurring. Different rewards are offered to users, which can range from financial rewards to the recognition of their work that users will participate.

From a business standpoint, it is important to understand:

- What is the logical scenario to implement a crowdsourcing initiative and also to understand their advantages and disadvantages.
- What are the steps that must be considered when launching an initiative like this:
  - The company identifies and clearly defines the problem to be solved;
  - It should raise the question and challenge the par4ticipants with the reward;
  - Work with the participants to energize and clarify doubts or unclear aspects;
  - The host provides ideas and proposals;
  - The company (or the participants themselves) chooses ideas considered as winners;
  - Rewarding the winner or winners;
  - Transfer (if so agreed) to the company the rights to use the ideas.
- What are the critical factors to take into account to make the initiative successful:
  - Clearly define what is expected;
  - Establish the proper reward, not just monetary;
  - Management of the community and building on ideas,
  - Selection process must be transparent and clear, ideally chosen by the group.

If you consider the main factors listed above and other factors which the company may consider necessary, they may be linked to the collective intelligence of a group to solve problems and innovate complex priority with a much greater diversity of opinion and paying only for what is considered as success.

To conclude the report, highlighting the role of crowdsourcing as a good catalyst for the innovation processes of companies, incorporating collective intelligence, open innovation and collaborative spirit in the task is not easy to adopt nowadays. The pioneers, who open new roads, will be those who are called to form this new partnership between all that lies ahead.

3.3 Conclusion

After analyzing the relationship between different environments, both corporate and university/research, to generate uptake and retention of users (both present and future) and ensure growth in the content generated by them, we note that for to uptake (and that recruiting users is one of the most important crowdsourcing challenges) exist five major solutions:

1. We can require users to make contributions if we have authority to do so (for example, a manager may require 100 employees to help build a company-wide system).
2. We can pay users. Mechanical Turk[4] for example provides a way to pay users on the web to help with a task.
3. We can ask for volunteers. This solution is free and easy to execute, and hence is most popular. Most current CS systems on the Web (such as Wikipedia, YouTube) use this solution. The downside of volunteering is that it is hard to predict how many users we can recruit for a particular application.
4. The fourth solution is to make users pay for service. The basic idea is to require the users of a system A to pay" for using A, by contributing to a CS system B. .....
5. The fifth solution is to piggyback on the user traces of a well-established system (such as building a spelling correction system by exploiting user traces of a search engine). This gives us a steady stream of users. But we must still solve the difficult challenge of determining how the traces can be exploited for our purpose.

Once we have selected a recruitment strategy, we should consider how to further encourage and retain users. Many encouragement and retention (E&R) schemes exist. We briefly discuss the most popular ones. First, we can provide instant gratification, by immediately showing a user how his or her contribution makes a difference. Second, we can provide an enjoyable experience or a necessary service, such as game playing (while making a contribution). Third, we can provide ways to establish, measure, and show fame/trust/ reputation. Fourth, we can set up competitions, such as showing top rated users. Finally, we can provide ownership situations, where a user may feel he or she "owns" a part of the system, and thus is compelled to "cultivate" that part. For example, zillow.com displays houses and estimates their market prices. It provides a way for a house owner to claim his or her house and provide the correct data (such as number of bedrooms), which in turn helps improve the price estimation.

These E&R schemes apply naturally to volunteering, but can also work well for other recruitment solutions. For example, after requiring a set of users to contribute, we can still provide instant gratification, enjoyable experience, fame management, and so on, to maximize user participation. Finally we note that deployed CS system often employ a mixture of recruitment methods (such as bootstrapping with "requirement" or "paying", then switching to "volunteering" once the system is sufficiently "mature").

4. Final conclusion

Many experts conclude that the crowdsourcing can be applied to a wide variety of problems, and that it raises numerous interesting technical and social challenges. Given the success of current CS systems, they expect that this emerging field will grow rapidly. In the near future, they foresee three major directions: more generic platforms, more applications and structure, and more users and complex contributions.

---

[4] The Amazon Mechanical Turk (MTurk) is a crowdsourcing Internet marketplace that enables computer programmers (known as *Requesters*) to co-ordinate the use of human intelligence to perform tasks that computers are unable to do yet.

First, the various systems built in the past decade have clearly demonstrated the value of crowdsourcing. The race is now on to move beyond building individual systems, toward building general CS platforms that can be used to develop such system quickly.

Second, they expect that crowdsourcing will be applied to ever more types of applications. Many of these applications will be formal and structured in some sense, making it easier to employ automatic techniques and to coordinate them with human users. In particular, a large chunk of the Web is about data and services. Consequently, they expect crowdsourcing to build structured database and structured services (Web services with formalized input and output) will receive increasing attention.

Finally, They expect many techniques will be developed to engage and ever broader range of users in crowdsourcing, and to enable them, especially naïve users, to make increasingly complex contributions, such as creating software programs and building mashups (without writing any code), and specifying complex structured data pieces (without knowing any structured query languages).

4.1 Final thoughts[5]

The networks have a life. They grow, change, reproduce, survive and die. A social network is a kind of super human, with an anatomy and physiology of their own. Social networks can develop a type of intelligence that increases or supplements individual intelligence.

5. Acknowledgments

To MIT Organization/Department: Douglas Morgenstern & Adolfo Plasencia URL: http://mitupv.mit.edu/
To AIMME: Santiago Bonet: http://www.metal20.org/

6. References

AIMME - Instituto Tecnológico Metalmecánico.(2011) El arte del crowdsourcing. http://metal20.org/crowds11.

AUI. La sociedad de la información en España (2006). 2007. http://aui.es/index.php?body=est_v1article&id_article=1947

La sociedad de la información en España (2010). Informes 2008.2009.2010.(11ª edición) http://sociedadinformacion.fundacion.telefonica.com/DYC/SHI/InformesSI/seccion=1190&idioma=es_ES.do

Baviera, T. ¿Qué aportan los blogs? (2007). http://www.conoze.com/doc.php?doc=7642

CAMPUS TECHNOLOGY, (2011)Students as Designers and Content Creators: An Online Multimedia Exchange between the U.S. and Spain http://campustechnology.com/Articles/2003/09/Students-as-Designers-and-Content-Creators-An-Online-Multimedia-Exchange-between-the-US-and-Spain.aspx

Carr, N. The amorality of Web 2.0. (2005). http://www.roughtype.com/archives/2005/10/the_amorality_o.php

Carr, N. (2003), "it doesn´t matter", Harvard business review.

Cornellá, A. (2005) Infoxicación. http://www.infonomia.com/blog/perm.php?id=2694

Christakis, Nicholas A., Fowler, James H. Connected. (2010).The suprising power of our Social Networks and How they shape our lives. Santillana.
Davey, D., Gade Jones, K. & Fox, J., (1995), "Multimedia for Language Learning: Some course design Issues", E-Journal article: Computer Assisted Language Learning, 8/1, pp.31-44
Dawson, R., (2007), Launching the web 2.0. Framework. (30-05-2007) http://www.rossdawsonblog.com/weblog/archives/2007/05/launching_the_w.html
Anhai Doan, Raghu Ramakishnan, & Alon Y.Halevy, (2011), Crowdsourcing systems on the world-wide web, Communications of the ACM (Vol.54, Issue 4, April 2011).
Ebersbach, A., Glaser, M., & Heigl, R. (2006). Wiki: Web collaboration. Germany: Springer-Verlag.
Fumero, A. & Genís, R. (2006), Web 2.0. Fundación Orange.
Gilchrist, A. (2007), "Can Web 2.0 be Used Effectively Inside Organisations?", Bilgi Dünyasý pp. 123-139.
Gonzalez A. (2011), Tu reputación en internet –Trei. http://antonio-gonzalez.info/ http://creoeninternet.com/antonio-gonzalez-reputacion-en-internet-trei/
Granovetter, M. (1973), "The strength of weak ties", American journal of sociology, vol. 78, pp. 1360-1380
Haworth, W. "The Internet as a Language Learning Resource." In Proceedings Eurocall ´95. Edited by A. Gimeno. Valencia: Universidad Politécnica de Valencia, 1995
Hewitt, A and Forte A,(2006) Crossing Boundaries: Identity Management and Student /Faculty Relationships on the Facebook, CSCW'06, November 4-8, 2006
Keen, A. (2007), The coult of the amateur. How today´s internet is killing our culture. Double Day. New York.
David Lazer, Alex (Sandy) Pentland, Lada Adamic, Sinan Aral, Albert Laszlo Barabasi, Devon Brewer, Nicholas Christakis, Noshir Contractor, James Fowler, Myron Gutmann, Tony Jebara, Gary King, Michael Macy, Deb Roy, and Marshall Van Alstyne David Lazer,(2009) Harvard University; Life in the network: the coming age of computational social science http://www.sciencemag.org/content/323/5915/721.short
Levy, M. (1997), Computer-Assisted Language Learning. Context and Conceptualization, Oxford: Clarendon Press, 1997
Levy, P. (2004), Inteligencia colectiva por una antropología del ciberespacio Organización panamericana de la salud. Washington, DC. http://inteligenciacolectiva.bvsalud.org
McAfee, A.(2006), "Enterprise 2.0: The Dawn of Emergent Collaboration", MIT Sloan management review, vol. 47, no. 3, pp. 21-28
McAfee, A.(2007b), The ties that find. 1-10-2007b. http://blog.hbs.edu/faculty/amcafee/index.php/faculty_amcafee_v3/the_ties_that_find/
McAfee, A.(2007a), How to hit the enterprise bulleye. 2007a. http://blog.hbs.edu/faculty/amcafee/index.php/faculty_amcafee_v3/how_to_hit_the_enterprise_20_bullseye/
Mckinsey Quarterly (2007), How businesses are using Web 2.0: A McKinsey Global Survey.
Mintzberg, H. (1973), The Nature of Managerial Work, Ed.Harper & Row.
MIT OPEN COURSE WARE.(2003) http://ocw.mit.edu/OcwWeb/Foreign-Languages-and-Literatures/21F-703Espanol-IIISpring2003/CourseHome/
MIT COMPARATIVE MEDIA STUDIES PROGRAM (2011) Applied Humanism

http://web.mit.edu/cms/Design/applied.html

Nunan, D.(1988), The Learner-centred Curriculum, Cambridge: Cambridge University Press, 1988

Pérez, L., The Effectiveness of Internet in the Foreign Language Classroom", Horizon http://horizon.unc.edu (2011/11)

Morris, M., Schindehutte, M., & Allen, J. (2005), "The entrepreneur's business model: toward a unified perspective", Journal of business research.

Orihuela, J. L. (2006), La revolución de los blogs. Cuando las bitácoras se convirtieron en el medio de comunicación de la gente. Ed.Madrid: la esfera de los libros.

O'Reilly, T.(2005) What is web 2.0 Design patterns and business models for the next generation of software. 2005. http://www.oreillynet.com/pub/a/oreilly/tim/news/2005/09/30/what-is-web-20.html

Rappa, M. digitalenterprise.(2007-2011). http://www.digitalenterprise.org

Dans, E. (2010), El mundo tras la Web 2.0 es más democrático, http://www.enriquedans.com/2010/11/el-mundo-tras-la-web-2-0-es-mas-democratico-en-diario-de-avisos.html

Dans, E., (2007), La empresa y la web 2.0. http://www.enriquedans.com/2007/06/la-empresa-y-la-web-20-articulo-en-harvard-deusto.html

Skehan, P. (1996), "Second Language Acquisition Research and Task-based Instruction", in Willis, J. & Willis, D. (eds.), *Challenge and Change in Language Teaching*, Oxford: Heinemann, 1996, p.20.

SYLLABUS. (2011) Students as Designers and Content Creators: An Online Multimedia Exchange between the U.S. and Spain. http://www.campus-technology.com/article.asp?id=8293

Web 2.0 in Wikipedia (English): http://en.wikipedia.org/wiki/Web_2

Anibal de la Torre (2006) Web Educativa 2.0, Edutec. Revista Electrónica de Tecnología Educativa, Núm. 20, Enero 06 http://www.uib.es/depart/gte/gte/edutec-e/revelec20/anibal20.htm

Widdowson, H. G. (1978), *Teaching Language as Communication,* Oxford: Oxford University Press, 1978.

Weinberger, D. (2007), Everything is miscellaneous. The Power of the New Digital Disorder Times Books. New York

Part 3

Multimedia Image Retrieval

5

Research Outline and Progress of Digital Protection on Thangka

Weilan Wang, Jianjun Qian and Xiaobao Lu
Northwest University for Nationalities, China

1. Introduction

"Thangka", is a transliteration of Tibetan which means painted scroll, an art of painting on silk or cloth. It is primary components of painting art in the snow-capped plateau with clear characteristics of Tibetan art, and has a long history, in the early 7th century when the Tubo dynasty had emerged, Buddhism are introduced Tibet. Extant the earliest Thangka is 11th century works, the most Thangka works are 17th century and 18th century, and all works that stored generation before the 15th century with little. Its content interesting and colorful stories, relate to religion, the history event, personage, local conditions and customs, folklore, fairy story, building layout, astronomy calendar, Tibetan medicine, Tibetan pharmacology and so on. It is extremely costful image data and historical material in Tibetan Studies field, and regarded as an encyclopedia of the history and society of the Tibetan ethnic group, having highly studying value and aesthetic value. The digital protection of Thangka is a very meaningful work with rapid development in information technology age. Thangka is the use of powder and drawn by the exquisite natural pigment paintings, and Thangka image different from the natural landscape images and other images due to its wide range of themes, the wide variety, different sorts, abstruse semantic, plump picture, brilliant color. So its research relate to image processing, pattern recognition, computer vision, artificial intelligence, etc.

Since 2002, our group relative research of Thangka image has been the State Ethnic Affairs Commission of China, the National Natural Science Foundation of China, Gansu Province Natural Science Foundation funding. So far, all aspects of research had made some progress, there are also many issues to be studied in further. Our study aim in the cultural heritage of Thangka is digital protection, main content include inpainting of Thangka image, construction of resource repository and information retrieval of Thangka, some research results will be introduced in this chapter.

The rest is organized as follows: Section 2 introduce restoration of Thangka image. Construction of recourse repository of Thangka is expressed in section 3. Thangka image annotation and retrieval semantic-based is introduced in section 4. In section 5, content-based Thangka image retrieval is introduced. Finally, the conclusions are drawn in section 6.

2. Restoration of Thangka image

2.1 Damaged Thangka and the meaning of digital restoration

Image inpainting is not only an important research topic in the fields of image restoration but also a research hotspot in image processing and computer vision. It's main application include virtual restoration of cultural heritage and artwork, region filling, object removal and so on [1,2,3,4,5,6,7]. Thangka as a living culture and an important cultural heritage, there are many treasures unique. But through the vicissitudes of life, some Thangka was serious damaged and the task of save, collation and study arduous will be very formidable. There is no doubt that improve the computer's processing capabilities in cultural heritage and artwork has important academic value, wide application of social and cultural development of great significance.

2.2 A digital restoration method for Thangka image

A new method is proposed for damaged image inpainting of Thangka image, which is combining the shape of damaged patches and type of neighborhood patches, according to the current algorithm characteristics of image inpainting, implementing automatic damaged regions inpainting.

2.2.1 Shape classification of damaged patches

The first stage is segmentation and merger. The initial segmentation is to get the damaged regions of image through watershed method [8], but it is prone to over-segmentation, therefore the region merging is used.

Small regions merging:

Step 1. transform original image from RGB to LUV;
Step 2. compute the LUV mean value of initial segmentation regions;
Step 3. get each neighborhood of segmentation regions;
Step 4. merge the small regions with it adjacently in space and similar in color;
Step 5. update LUV mean value and neighborhood information of each small regions, up till inexistence the small region of area less than threshold Ta;

Regions are merged to color close and space adjoins:

Step 1. compute the squared error of each small region with its neighborhood in LUV space;
Step 2. judge whether exist neighborhood patches that less than threshold Ts in the squared error, if present, then current small will be merged to the area of the least squared error, if not, do nothing;
Step 3. operate by repeated merging, until without the regions can be merged.

Through the above merger can restrain over-segmentation or less-segmentation effectively, where area threshold Ta and squared error threshold Ts need to be repetitious adjusted.

The next stage is shape classification of damaged patches.

Obtain the damaged patches. A mask image can be obtained through the damaged region segmentation, where each pixel is represent with 1 for damaged region and each pixel is represent with 0 for non-damaged region. Assumptions the mask image of damaged region segmented as showing in Fig 1, the algorithm to get the damaged patches by region growing steps are:

Step 1. along the scanning line direction to scan the mask image, to initialize the mark of damaged patches: $sign = 2$;

Step 2. Step 2. if the pixel value is 1,then the node add FIFO (First Input First Output), and the node value is updated to $sign = 2$;

Step 3. Step 3. pop-up the first elements in the FIFO, make 4-neighbour or 8-neighbour region growing, if the pixel value of neighborhood is 1,then add FIFO, and its value is updated to $sign$, otherwise, do nothing, up till the FIFO is empty;

Step 4. Step 4. $sign++$, repeat Step 2 and Step 3, until the scanning finish all pixels of the whole image.

In order to prevent the confusion for damaged patches sign and damaged pixel mark, initialize $sign = 2$, all damaged patches sign will subtract 1 while find each damaged patches, and made the first damaged patches mark 1, The second damaged patches mark 2, and so on, the k damaged patches mark k. The pixel-set of pixel value 1 and 2 is mark of damaged patches and its number respectively, Fig 2 is damaged patches mark of Fig 1.

0	0	0	0	0	0	0	0	0	0	0	0	0	0	0	0	0	0	0	0
0	0	0	0	0	0	0	0	0	0	0	0	0	0	0	0	0	0	0	0
0	1	1	1	1	1	1	1	1	1	1	1	1	1	1	1	0	0	0	0
0	1	1	1	1	1	1	1	1	1	1	1	1	1	1	0	0	0	0	0
0	0	0	0	0	0	0	1	0	0	0	0	0	0	0	0	0	0	0	0
0	0	0	0	0	0	0	0	0	0	0	0	0	0	0	0	0	0	0	0
0	0	0	0	0	0	0	0	0	0	0	0	0	0	0	0	0	0	0	0
0	0	0	0	0	0	0	0	0	0	0	0	0	0	0	0	0	0	0	0
0	1	1	1	1	1	1	1	1	1	1	1	0	0	0	0	0	0	0	0
0	1	1	1	1	1	1	1	1	1	1	0	0	0	0	0	0	0	0	0
0	1	1	1	1	1	1	1	1	1	1	0	0	0	0	0	0	0	0	0
0	0	0	0	0	0	0	0	1	1	1	1	1	0	0	0	0	0	0	0
0	0	0	0	0	0	0	0	1	1	1	1	1	0	0	0	0	0	0	0
0	0	0	0	0	0	0	0	1	1	1	1	1	0	0	0	0	0	0	0
0	0	0	0	0	0	0	0	1	1	1	1	1	0	0	0	0	0	0	0
0	0	0	0	0	0	0	0	1	1	1	1	1	0	0	0	0	0	0	0
0	0	0	0	0	0	0	0	0	0	0	0	0	0	0	0	0	0	0	0
0	0	0	0	0	0	0	0	0	0	0	0	0	0	0	0	0	0	0	0
0	0	0	0	0	0	0	0	0	0	0	0	0	0	0	0	0	0	0	0
0	0	0	0	0	0	0	0	0	0	0	0	0	0	0	0	0	0	0	0

Fig. 1. The mask image of damaged region

0	0	0	0	0	0	0	0	0	0	0	0	0	0	0	0	0	0	0	0
0	0	0	0	0	0	0	0	0	0	0	0	0	0	0	0	0	0	0	0
0	1	1	1	1	1	1	1	1	1	1	1	1	1	1	1	0	0	0	0
0	1	1	1	1	1	1	1	1	1	1	1	1	1	1	0	0	0	0	0
0	0	0	0	0	0	0	1	0	0	0	0	0	0	0	0	0	0	0	0
0	0	0	0	0	0	0	0	0	0	0	0	0	0	0	0	0	0	0	0
0	0	0	0	0	0	0	0	0	0	0	0	0	0	0	0	0	0	0	0
0	0	0	0	0	0	0	0	0	0	0	0	0	0	0	0	0	0	0	0
0	2	2	2	2	2	2	2	2	2	2	2	0	0	0	0	0	0	0	0
0	2	2	2	2	2	2	2	2	2	2	0	0	0	0	0	0	0	0	0
0	2	2	2	2	2	2	2	2	2	2	0	0	0	0	0	0	0	0	0
0	0	0	0	0	0	0	0	2	2	2	2	2	0	0	0	0	0	0	0
0	0	0	0	0	0	0	0	2	2	2	2	2	0	0	0	0	0	0	0
0	0	0	0	0	0	0	0	2	2	2	2	2	0	0	0	0	0	0	0
0	0	0	0	0	0	0	0	2	2	2	2	2	0	0	0	0	0	0	0
0	0	0	0	0	0	0	0	2	2	2	2	2	0	0	0	0	0	0	0
0	0	0	0	0	0	0	0	0	0	0	0	0	0	0	0	0	0	0	0
0	0	0	0	0	0	0	0	0	0	0	0	0	0	0	0	0	0	0	0
0	0	0	0	0	0	0	0	0	0	0	0	0	0	0	0	0	0	0	0
0	0	0	0	0	0	0	0	0	0	0	0	0	0	0	0	0	0	0	0

Fig. 2. Damaged patches mark of damaged patches

Shape classify to damaged patches. Studies show that the width or height of damaged patches can be repaired is T on non-texture structure inpainting algorithms, its range between 30 and 40. Moreover, texture structure inpainting algorithms can repair damaged image in a larger scale. Linear classifier as formula (1):

$$f(x) = \min(Mw, Mh) - T \quad (1)$$

Where, min mean lesser, Mw and Mh denote width and height of the damaged patches, T indicate the maximum width or height that can be inpainted damaged patches for the method of non-texture structure; the damaged patches is linear while $f(x) < 0$, and the damaged patches is blocky while $f(x) \geq 0$.

2.2.2 Neighborhood classification of damaged patches

Image segmentation make whole image divided into mutually disjoint regions, texture information of neighborhood must be obtained when neighborhood classification of damaged patches. The situation of the neighborhood of damaged patches is roughly: (1) the around of damaged patches is texture region; (2) the around of damaged patches is non-texture region; (3) the around of damaged patches is mixed region, that is, have both texture region and non-texture region. Fig 3 is a schematic drawing that image segmented, where A, B and C is neighborhood patches of damaged patches.

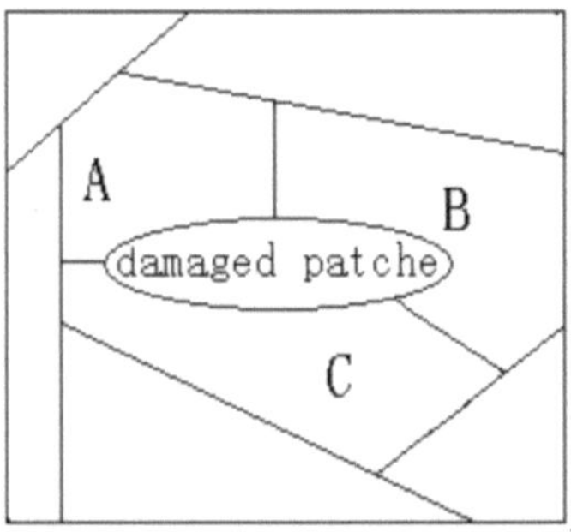

Fig. 3. Neighborhood patches

The algorithms of acquiring the neighborhood patches of damaged patches as following:

Step 1. get the outer-edge's mark of damaged patches, outer-edge is non-damaged pixels and inner-edge is damaged pixels;

Step 2. reject the iterative mark of edge, the remaining mark is the neighborhood's number of damaged patches;

Step 3. use the remaining mark as kernel points, adopt the method of region growing to get the neighborhood patches of damaged patches.

The current image inpainting algorithms are divided into two primary categories: texture and non-texture, therefore the neighborhood patches of damaged patches will be divided into: texture patches and non-texture patches, so that selection corresponding algorithm to repair a damaged image.

We use gray level co-occurrence matrix to extract two-order statistics information, and then extract texture feature of image.

Gray level co-occurrence matrix:

For any given a 2D image $f(x,y)$, and gray level Ng, then the size of gray level co-occurrence matrix is $Ng \times Ng$, each element of the matrix is defined by (2):

$$p(i,j)=\frac{\#\{[(x_1,y_1),(x_2,y_2)]\in S\mid f(x_1,y_1)=i,f(x_2,y_2)=j\}}{\#S} \tag{2}$$

Where, # denote the frequency of pixel point that satisfies some condition; (x_1,y_1) and (x_2,y_2) is space coordinate of pixel points, respectively; S expresses the set of pixel pair that have something space relation; i and j indicate gray value of pixel.

Due to symmetry properties of gray level co-occurrence matrix, generally only need to calculate in four direction: 0^0 , 45^0 , 90^0 and 135^0 respectively, and make finally features that have rotational invariance. Texture size is different for different texture image, also different on gray level co-occurrence matrix, therefore the various statistics of gray level co-occurrence matrix as texture features. Those statistics are angular second-order moment, contrast, relevance, entropy and inverse difference moment, respectively.

Angular second-order moment:

$$F_1=\sum_{i=0}^{Ng-1}\sum_{j=0}^{Ng-1}p^2(i,j) \tag{3}$$

F_1 reflect the local uniformity of image, the bigger is the value, the more uniform is image texture; otherwise indicates the image have many transition level. Contrast:

$$F_2=\sum_{n=0}^{Ng-1}n^2\sum_{i=0}^{Ng-1}\sum_{j=0}^{Ng-1}p(i,j) \tag{4}$$

F_2 reflect the local variance of image, the value smaller for coarse texture, and the value larger for fine texture. If image is uniformity then F_2 equal to 0. Relevance:

$$F_3=\sum_{i=0}^{Ng-1}\sum_{j=0}^{Ng-1}\frac{ijp(i,j)-u_xu_y}{\sigma_x^2\sigma_y^2} \tag{5}$$

Where, $u_x=\sum_{n=0}^{Ng-1}i\sum_{i=0}^{Ng-1}\sum_{j=0}^{Ng-1}p(i,j)$, $u_y=\sum_{n=0}^{Ng-1}j\sum_{i=0}^{Ng-1}\sum_{j=0}^{Ng-1}p(i,j)$, $\sigma_x^2=\sum_{i=0}^{Ng-1}(i-u_x)^2\sum_{j=0}^{Ng-1}p(i,j)$, $\sigma_y^2=\sum_{j=0}^{Ng-1}(j-u_y)^2\sum_{i=0}^{Ng-1}p(i,j)$. F_3 is similarity measurement between rows and columns in gray level co-occurrence matrix, which reflect the depends linearly relationship of gray. Entropy:

$$F_4=-\sum_{i=0}^{Ng-1}\sum_{j=0}^{Ng-1}p(i,j)\lg p(i,j) \tag{6}$$

F_4 reflect the complexity of texture, the more complication is the texture, the more higher is the entropy; otherwise tend to low entropy. Inverse difference moment:

$$F_5=\sum_{i=0}^{Ng-1}\sum_{j=0}^{Ng-1}\frac{p(i,j)}{[1+(i-j)^2]} \tag{7}$$

F_5 is the reverse of contrast on gray level co-occurrence matrix, which measure the local consistency of image. If an image is approach uniform, the inverse difference moment tend to 1.

Calculate angular second-order moment, contrast, relevance, entropy and inverse difference moment in four direction: 0^0, 45^0, 90^0 and 135^0, respectively, their expectation and variance as final features.

The size and rang of texture features is different, they are called heterogeneous feature, and need normalization process. Assuming there are M samples, features of each sample expressed as: $(u_{Fi1}, u_{Fi2}, u_{Fi3}, u_{Fi4}, u_{Fi5}, \sigma_{Fi1}, \sigma_{Fi2,}, \sigma_{Fi3}, \sigma_{Fi4}, \sigma_{Fi5})$, where $1 \le i \le M$. Take one of the feature components for example, our improved Gauss normalization as following:

Let u_{F1j}, u_{F2j}, ..., u_{FMj} indicate the j dimension feature components of M samples, u_{Fj} and σ_{Fj} denote expectation and variance respectively. The feature u_{Fij} can be normalized in $(0,1)$ by formula (8) which play role is identical for each component.

$$N(u_{Fij}) = \frac{\frac{u_{Fij} - u_{Fj}}{3\sigma_{Fj}} + 1}{2} \tag{8}$$

The following is classification method of damaged neighbourhood.

Main inpainting algorithm generally is classified into two categories: structure-based inpainting and texture-based inpainting. The neighborhood patches of damaged patches are divided into texture, non-texture and mixed in our study, so that farther to select different algorithm to repair damaged patches according as they neighborhood patches. On the basis of the feature extraction of neighborhood patches make neighborhood classification of damaged patches, k-nearest neighborhood(KNN) method were taking place to classify neighborhood patches.

The classification on neighborhood patches of damaged patches based on feature of neighborhood patches. Suppose that there are M training samples, where, N1 belongs to texture category ω_1, N_2 belongs to non-texture category ω_2, and N_1+N_2 =M. Now an unknown category sample X, X belongs to ω_1 or belongs to ω_2? k-nearest neighborhood method is just to compute the distances between the X's feature and M training sample's feature, and then sort the distances from small to big, to take the smaller K distances, and K is odd number. Finally, according to the category labeled of the smaller K distances vote to get the unknown sample's category labels. The vote method is: if the number more belong to ω_1 in the K samples, then X belongs to ω_1, otherwise X belongs to ω_2. Where $K = 9$, which is determined by following experiment.

There are 100 training samples, 50 non-texture images and 50 texture images, 40 test samples include 20 non-texture images and 20 texture images. At first, extract feature of training samples through the previous methods, and then calculate the recognition rat of different K, at last, select an appropriate K. Table 1 is the results of experiment.

Table 1 shows: when K increasing, recognition rate is rising gradually, recognition rate have reached plateau when K soared to 9. Therefore K=9 is better, this not only avoided a lot of similarity calculation, but also can decrease the number of training samples and save memory space.

K	Recognition rate of non-texture	Recognition rate of texture	General recognition rate
1	70%	80%	75%
3	80%	90%	85%
5	90%	90%	90%
7	90%	90%	90%
9	100%	90%	95%
11	100%	90%	95%
21	100%	90%	95%
51	100%	90%	95%

Table 1. The recognition rate with different K for neighborhood classified of damaged patches

2.2.3 Restoration the damaged patches

Restoration method is founded on algorithm analysis, shape of damaged patches and neighborhood type, at same time, the type of damaged patches is established through its neighborhood. Combining shape of damaged patches, the type of neighborhood patches can achieve algorithm's automatic selection when restoration a damaged image.

The proceedings will begin with, to construct algorithms library for Thangka image. There are four algorithms in algorithms library: design and implementation of algorithm 1 depending on the current exemplar-based image inpainting [7]; sampled-based texture synthesis be called algorithm 2 by [9,10]; algorithm 3 be designmed by the Oliveira model [6]; and algorithm 4 is finished by TV or CDD model [2,3].

Secondly, algorithms are automatic selected based on the shape and type of damaged patches. The type of damaged patches based on the neighborhood are given in the form of define.

Define 1. If the damaged patches have one neighborhood patches of non-feature, the type is called *damaged patches of homogeneous non-feature.*
Define 2. If the damaged patches have more than one neighborhood patches of non-feature, the type is called *damaged patches of heterogeneity non-feature.*
Define 3. If the damaged patches have more than one neighborhood patches of feature and non-feature, the type is called *damaged patches of mixed type.*
Define 4. If the damaged patches have one neighborhood patches of feature, the type is called *damaged patches of homogeneous feature.*
Define 5. If the damaged patches have more than one neighborhood patches of feature, the type is called *damaged patches of heterogeneity feature.*

Fig.4 shows our research result to select inpainting algorithm according to damaged patches shape and neighborhood type of damaged patches.

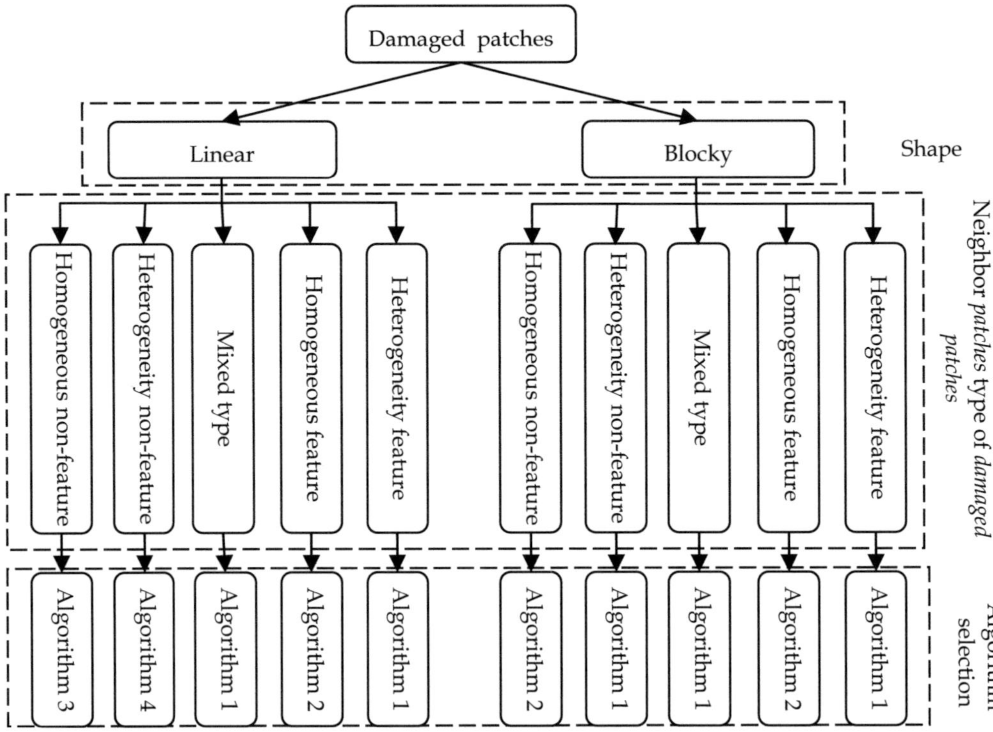

Fig. 4. Algorithm selection according to damaged patches shape and neighborhood type

Finally, inpainting process of damaged Thangka image based on damaged patches shape, neighborhood patches of damaged patches, characteristics of current inpainting algorithm, are given in the form of flow graph in Fig.5.

Through damaged region segmentation to get damaged patches, the reaction process is as follows when number of damaged patches is not equal to 0.

If the shape of damaged patches is linear, inpainting the damaged patches with Algorithm 1 when the neighborhood is heterogeneity feature or mixed type; inpainting the damaged patches with Algorithm 2 when the neighborhood of damaged patches is heterogeneity non-feature; inpainting the damaged patches with Algorithm 3 when the neighborhood is homogeneous non-feature; inpainting the damaged patches with Algorithm 4 when the neighborhood is heterogeneity non-feature.

If the shape of damaged patches is blocky, inpainting the damaged patches with Algorithm 1 when the neighborhood is heterogeneity feature, heterogeneity non-feature or mixed type; inpainting the damaged patches with Algorithm 2 when the neighborhood is homogeneous feature or homogeneous non-feature.

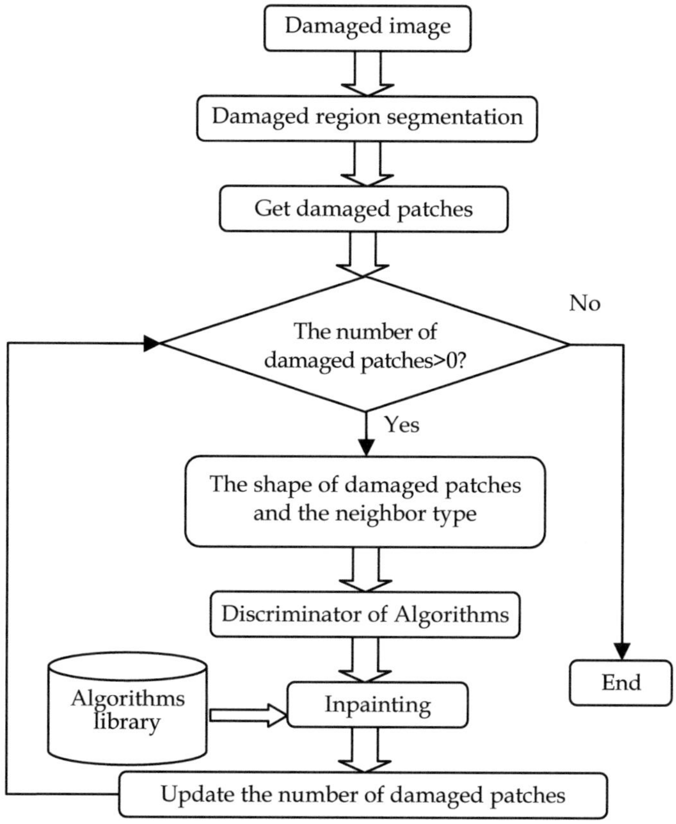

Fig. 5. Flow graph of inpainting process

2.3 Inpainting effect of damaged Thangka images

Some original damaged Thangka images show in Fig 6a, 6c, 6e on the left , Fig 6b, 6d, 6f on the right are corresponding inpainted results.

Fig. 7 shows some non-natural damaged Thangka images and their inpainted results.

In our research, experiment and analysis demonstrate:

1. Inpainting effect to non-natural damaged Thangka images was superior to natural damaged Thangka images.
2. Precision of selection algorithm is 80% which are affected by precision of neighborhood patches classified, correctness of segmentation damaged regions, and accuracy of damaged patches shape, however, segmentation is a predominant influence in the problem.

2.4 The current conclusion

1. In recent years, we have carried out research on this issue with related model of image inpainting, inpainting algorithm etc. [11,12], the study provides basis for this chapter in inpainting area of Thangka image.

(a) Damaged image (b) Inpainted image

(c) Damaged image (d) Inpainted image

(e) Damaged image (f) Inpainted image

Fig. 6. Damaged Thangka images (local)

(a) Original image (b) Damaged image (c) Inpainted image

(d) Original image (e) Damaged image (f) Inpainted image

(g) Original image (h) Damaged image (i) Inpainted image

Fig. 7. Damaged Thangka images (local)

2. Improve and achieve current inpainting algorithm in Thangka image domain, these algorithm including exemplar-based inpainting algorithm, sampled-based texture synthesis algorithm, the algorithm based on the Oliveira model, CDD and TV model and so on.
3. The classification problem of damaged patches shapes was studied.
4. The classification of the neighborhood patches of damaged patches was studied, and damaged image was segmented by watershed algorithm in order to facilitate access to the adjacent information of damaged patches.

5. Implemented the automatic selection of inpainting algorithms combining the characteristics of different inpainting algorithms, the shape of damaged patches and the type of neighborhood patches.

There are a lot of correlative repair problem to need solution in damaged Thangka image, such as damaged region segmentation, obtaining damaged patches accurately, and effective inpainting the damaged patches. Main challenges for 2-D image inpainting lie in three aspects: domain complexity, image complexity and pattern complexity. Compared with all other image inpainting problems, for example, removal of occlusions, inpainting of old photographs, Thangka image's inpainting will be more difficulty due to the complexity of picture in the artwork domain. Furthermore, image segmentation of complex damaged and appropriate to Thangka image inpainting algorithm.

3. Construction of recourse repository of Thangka

This part researches on image knowledge repository for Thangka image based on the high level semantic about the attributes that describe the mains in the pictures. The attributes of mains are the domain knowledge that uses to establish the repository exactly, such as mains' name, headwear, appearance, complexion, mudra, talisman etc. Firstly, devise the conceptual data model of describing the mains depending on the attributes, show with relational schema of relational database. Secondly, build image libraries on the basis of the kinds, in accordance with the relational schema, use the non-automatic way acquiring knowledge, that is, devise a special knowledge editor to get knowledge, form various fact base for the kinds of mains and obtain fact knowledge for the repository. Thirdly, select some attributes that can typically distinguish mains depending on the characteristics of the mains attributes as key attributes, adopt production rule knowledge representation method, save the key attributes to be conditions and names of mains to be conclusions, form rule knowledge for the repository. At last, connect facts and rules by the process of knowledge query, combine forward reasoning control, and split strategies base in the light of the attribute of headwear, shape hierarchical conditions for production rule depending on execution sequence of key attributes for every strategy, take Structure Query Language of relational database to finish the reasoning work, provide strategy and rules in the process of reasoning and semantic introductions about the result image for users, construct Thangka image knowledge repository.

3.1 Attribute database of Thangka image

Thangka are generally classified into five areas by the content of picture: all kinds of deities, human figures, Gesar, science and technology (building layout, astronomy calendar, Tibetan medicine, Tibet pharmacology), decorative pattern and so on. Take for case of religion, according to the status and identity of the main in Tibetan Buddhism culture, they have several kinds of them, including Buddha, Patriarch, Bodhisattva, Yidam, Buddha Mother, Arhat, Dakini, Dharmapala, Genius God and so on. The attributes of mains are the domain knowledge that uses to establish the repository exactly, such as main Buddha's name, headwear, appearance, complexion, mudra, talisman etc.

Fig 8a, 8b, 8c, 8d, 8e, 8f, 8g is Amitabha Pure Land, Songzan Ganbu, Jokhang, Gesar, The universe, Medical, The auspicious designs, they belong to seven categories: deities, human figures, Gesar, building, astronomy calendar, Tibetan medicine, decorative pattern, respectively. Where, Fig 8h is a damaged Thangka image of local Yellow Kubera.

Fig. 8. Different classes of Thangka image

For example, take the Buddha. Attribute of Buddha category: appearance, complexion, headwear, pendant, dress, left-mudra, right-mudra, left-gesture, right-gesture, seat stand, setting posture, head light, back light, offerings, denominations, producing method, materials, works style, age, author, etc. they attribute values are identified as follows:

Appearance: anger, calm, less-huffish.
Complexion: yellow, red, blue, white and green.
Headwear: crown, bun, golden-crown, five-leaf-crown.
Pendant: treasure necklace, treasure rucaka, twin treasure necklace.
Dress: necklace of jade and pearls, cassock, Amai Mitsu.
Left or right-hand-mudra: mudra of teaching, dhyana-mudra, bhumisparsha-mudra, dharmacakra-mudra, varada, abhaya-mudra, lotus bud-mudra, mingwang-mudra.
Talisman: padma, prayer beads, dharma-cakra, bowl, sword, ten spoke wheel, spike flag, scape, net bottle, gold bottle, evergreen baoshu, saraca indica, flame ring wheel, vajra pestle, vajra rope, kancana-mandala.

Seat stand: padmasana throne, lion throne, padmasana and sun and moon disk, peacock throne, elephant throne.
Sitting posture: sitting meditation, hero posture, heroine posture, game posture, maharaja game posture, padmasana hero posture, vajra posture.
Head light color: green, black, red, transparence, orange.
Back light: yellow light disk, blue light disk, yellow and blue light disk, transparence, blue and red and yellow light disk, color light disk, green light disk, red light disk, gray light disk.

Offerings: bowl, fruit, padma, kapala bowl, aquarius, conch, jewellery, water, mirror, piano, cymbals, flute, milk, silk ribbon, Buddhist law wheel.

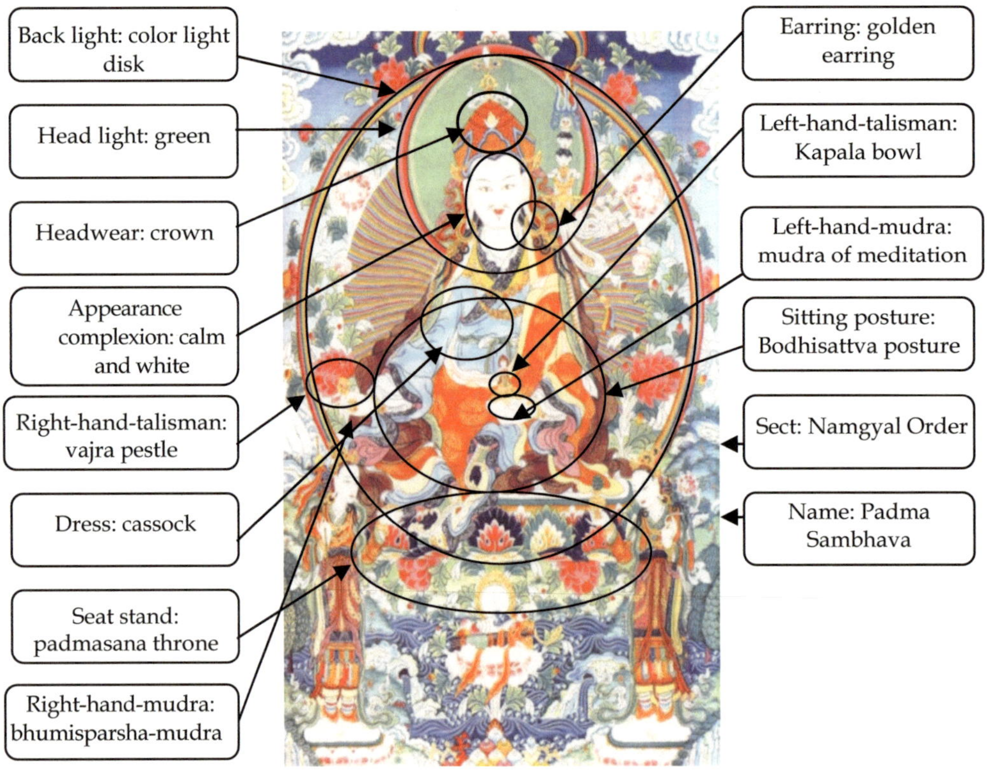

Fig. 9. Main attribute and attribute value

Sect: Namgyal Order, Sakya Order, Kadam Order, Kargyu Order, Gelukpa Order.
Production method: painting, barbola, embroidery, tapestry, appliqué, seed stitch, forme.
Materials: paper, cloth, shortening, timber, metal, stone.
Age: before sixteenth century, seventeenth century, eighteenth century, and after nineteenth century, unspecified.
The different category have different attribute item and attribute value. For instance, Fig. 9 show Padma Sambhava's main attribute and attribute value for masters type.

3.2 Knowledge repository's basic construction

There are sixe basic components in the knowledge repository of Thangka image:

1. Fundamental knowledge base. It is memory machine of factual knowledge and regularity knowledge
2. Knowledge reasoning. Inference mechanism is a set program that is used to control and coordination the knowledge base system, which derive the corresponding conclusion according to the fact and date of external input which are date of integrated database and fundamental knowledge base, by some inference strategy.
3. Interface of knowledge acquisition. Acquisition the domain knowledge from knowledge source to create fundamental knowledge base include fact and rule, the purpose of knowledge acquisition is to translate expert's domain knowledge for representation and reasoning of computer.
4. User interface. It is interface to achieve information exchange of knowledge base and outside.
5. Integrated database. it is working memory of knowledge base, which save with to be solved issue related initial conditions, fact, date, the various intermediate conclusions in reasoning process, objective conclusion etc.
6. Explanation mechanism. Its function is to provide rules and strategies in the process of knowledge reasoning aimed at query condition of user.

The core parts of the knowledge repository are fundamental knowledge base and inference mechanism. Knowledge repository's basic structure show in Fig 10.

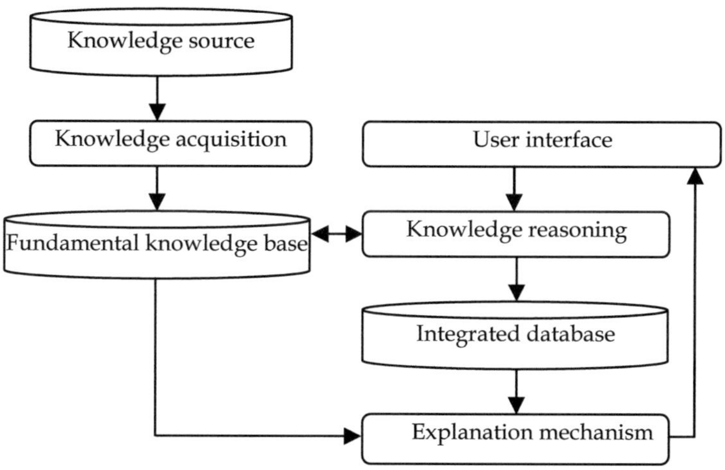

Fig. 10. Knowledge repository's basic structure

Interface of knowledge acquisition in Chinese, Fig.11 is the interface of selection of type, Fig.12 is the interface of knowledge input for Bodhisattva, some attribute value can be obtain through direct input or selection of drop-down menu.

Take for case of Buddha:

1. Select some attributes that can typically distinguish main Buddha depending on the characteristics of the main Buddha attributes as key elements, adopt knowledge representation method of production rule, save the key elements to be conditions and name of main Buddha to be conclusions, form rule knowledge for the repository.

Fig. 11. Interface of knowledge acquisition of selection type

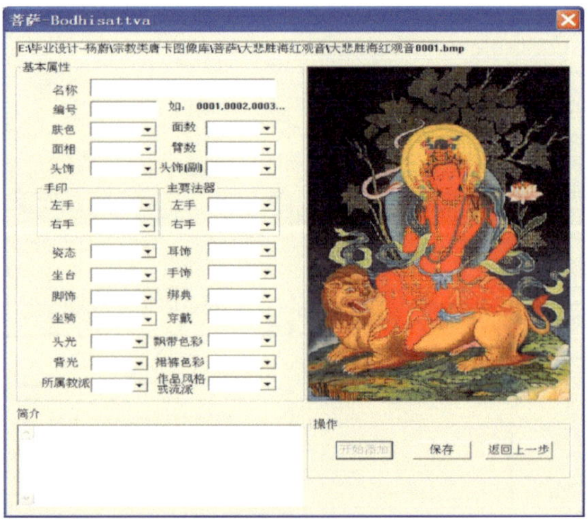

Fig. 12. Interface of knowledge input for Bodhisattva

2. Connect facts and rules by the process of knowledge query, combine forward reasoning control, and split strategies base in the light of the attribute of headwear, shape hierarchical conditions for production rule depending on execution sequence of key attributes for every strategy, take Structure Query Language of relational database to finish the reasoning work, provide strategy and rules in the process of reasoning and semantic introductions about the result image for users, eventually construct the Tibetan Buddhism Thangka Image Knowledge Repository.

Where, regularity knowledge is described by produce representation method of cause and effect, its basis form: IF conditions THEN Conclusions, which means is if the condition is satisfied, then can launch the corresponding conclusion. Take image's attributes as condition portion and the image as results section, and identify main Buddha by its title. Take the case of Sakyamuni Buddha, produce representation method of knowledge describe the connection of image and attributes, the rule as below:

IF	Headwear = bun	AND
	Appearance= calm	AND
	Complexion= yellow	AND
	Left-hand-talisman=bowl	AND
	Left-hand-mudra= meditation mudra	AND
	Right-hand-mudra= bhumisparsha-mudra	AND
	Dress=cassock	AND
	Sitting posture= meditation	AND
	Seat stand= padmasana throne	
THEN	Sakyamuni Buddha	

4. Thangka image annotation and retrieval semantic-based

4.1 The meaning and tasks of Thangka image annotation

It is the need of semantic-based Thangka image retrieval to establish an artifact annotation Thangka image database in a more object-oriented world. Thangka image annotation will be a heavy task with different classification, different content, and a picture with a lot of objects.

4.2 The current annotation methods and annotation contents

Take for case of religion of the main in Tibetan Buddhism [13,14]:

1. A headdress feature expression approach which mainly used contour feature and color feature are proposed. The average of spectral frequency represents contour feature. The color moment of internal contour represents color feature. Meanwhile, we can automatically annotate headdress concepts through computing variable quantity of spectral frequency and analyzing color distribution of internal contour.
2. A gesture feature expression method including five fingers directions, palm direction, relate position of gesture is presented. Because of the difficult features for segmenting gestures of Thangka image. Then, the concepts of unknown gestures can be predicted with nearest neighborhood method on the basis of training annotated gesture set.

4.3 Semantic retrieval framework of Thangka image

The process of semantic-based Thangka image retrieval includes five steps: (1) Identifying ROI (region of interested) of Thangka image; (2) Extracting visual features of ROI; (3) Training concepts classifier with concept dictionary and visual features; (4) Constructing C-K relation net; (5) Obtaining the retrieval result through using CSM algorithm on the basis of C-K relation net. This research focuses on step (4) and (5).

4.4 Construct C-K relation net

C-K relation net is a description to the membership degree of semantic keyword and relativity between semantic keywords as shown in Fig. 13; the lines between c_i (any conception node) and k_j (any keyword node) indicate the membership degree between conceptions of keywords, the lines between k_j node denote the relationship of keywords, and the lines of same color indicate the keywords are correlative. The membership degree of some keywords belonging to a concept can be computed by the method of combining the Delphi method and fuzzy statistics, after artificial annotation to ensure the relativity between keyword and keyword. For example, the keywords "wisdom", "sword of wisdom" and "enlightenment" belong to the concept "Sword", and the membership degree which can be computed by subsequent methods are 0.45,1 and 0.85 respectively. Moreover, the keyword "wisdom" also belongs to concepts "Rosary", "padma", "Bow and Arrow", and so on[15].

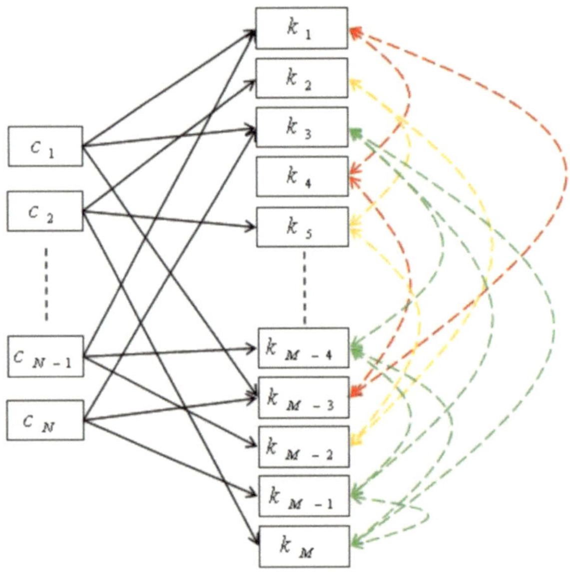

Fig. 13. *C-K* relation net

Suppose $E_{i,j}$ is membership degree of the *jth* keyword to the *ith* concept, then $E_{i,j}$ can be calculated:

$$E_{i,j} = \frac{\omega_1 D_{i,j} + \omega_2 F_{i,j}}{\omega_1 + \omega_2} \tag{9}$$

where $D_{i,j}$ indicate the membership degree of the *ith* keyword to the *jth* concept by the Delphi method, $F_{i,j}$ is the membership degree of the *jth* keyword to *ith* concept by fuzzy statistics, ω_1 and ω_2 are weighing coefficient.

The Delphi method, named by an ancient Greece city Delphi, is an expert survey of established procedure. Since 40s in 20th, it has been widely used in several fields such as economic management, psychology, sociology and so on. The characteristic of the Delphi method is concentrating the experience and advices of experts, to obtain the satisfying results by constantly feedback and revises. Semantic keyword is a description to conception in Thangka image, at the same time the membership degree of keyword to conception is different, besides, the emphasis to understand concepts is also different in various painting school. Therefore, we adopt the Delphi method to calculate membership degree between semantic keyword and concept in this paper.

Supposed there are n domain experts, then $m_{i,j}^{k}(k=1,2,\cdots n)$ indicate the membership degree of jth keyword to ith concept for someone expert's opinion. The average value of the membership degree can be calculated by (10), where a_k represents the weight of kth expert.

$$\overline{m_{i,j}} = \sum_{k=1}^{n} a_k m_{i,j}^{k} \tag{10}$$

And , the deviation $m_{i,j}^{k}$ can be calculated by formula (11):

$$d = \sum_{k=1}^{n} a_k \left| m_{i,j}^{k} - \overline{m_{i,j}} \right| \tag{11}$$

To given error $\varepsilon > 0$, if $d \leq \varepsilon$, then $\overline{m_{i,j}}$ as an approximate value of $D_{i,j}$; if $d > \varepsilon$, then repeat the above process, until the precision is satisfied. Here $\varepsilon = 0.19$

By statistic of the frequency of every semantic keyword appearing in the concepts and the method of membership functions mentioned above, we can calculate the membership degree of the semantic keyword to the concept.

In Thangka images, some semantic keywords are exclusive word to describe a concept, so the membership degree of the semantic keyword to the concept is high. On the other hand, some semantic keywords (including the ones have similar semantic) appear in several concepts, and then the membership degree of the semantic keyword to the concept is low. Based on the above characteristics, we propose a membership function as following:

$$F_{i,j} = \begin{cases} 1 & x_{i,j} = 1 \\ \dfrac{1}{x_{i,j}} + \beta & x_{i,j} \geq 1 \end{cases} \tag{12}$$

Where $x_{i,j}$ is a frequency of the ith concept corresponding the jth keyword (include with similarity semantic keywords) in all concepts, β is correction parameter. The membership degree of jth keyword to ith concept decreases with the increasing of $x_{i,j}$, despite the decreasing of inverse proportion function $\frac{1}{x}$ satisfies this relationship, it does not reflect the membership degree of keywords to concepts in quantity. Without correction parameter β, while $x_{i,j} = 2$, $F_{i,j} = 0.5$ indicates the description of membership degree of two keywords to ith concept, it is incorrect obviously. In this kind of situations, the membership degree is comparatively high. Therefore, correction parameter β is introduced to make the degree of membership function could more accurately reflect the degree of keywords to the concepts.

4.5 CSM algorithm

The main idea of CSM algorithm is to utilize membership relation of semantic keywords and concept, relativity of semantic keywords, to calculate the similarity. The procedures are as follows:

Step 1. in descending order, rank the membership degree of the semantic keyword which C_k is corresponding to.
Step 2. search whether there are $C_{k,j}$ in other concepts or those have similar semantic to $C_{k,j}$ in *C-K* relation net, if done, then ordinal execute, or else turn to Step 4.
Step 3. extract $C_{k,j}$ appear in other concepts and those keywords have similar semantic to $C_{k,j}$, then from high to low, rank the membership degree of the concepts which the semantic keyword are corresponding to. Save the concepts to RC .
Step 4. determine whether the searching of semantic keyword corresponding to C_k is over. If done, then the arithmetic is over, or else turns to Step 2.

Where, C_k represents the concept waiting to be retrieved, $C_{k,j}$ represents the jth keyword corresponding to the kth concept, $E_{k,j}$ represents specific degree that the jth keyword subordinate to kth concept, and RC represents the set of similarity concepts which are retrieved finally. On the basis of *C-K* relation net, applying CSM algorithm to measure the similarity of concepts could meet the retrieval needs of customers better. Because this algorithm leans on *C-K* relation net, thereby, the efficiency of CSM algorithm will be influenced by the dilatation of *C-K* relation net.

4.6 Semantic-based retrieval

Semantic-based Thangka image retrieval was roughly classified into three layers in our research: (1) it is similarities of visual features that receive most attention on visual layer; (2) it towards coherence of key area's concept on concept layer; (3) high level semantic retrieval place more weight on similarities of concepts. The experiment show that different retrieval layers can meet different users' demand and outcome is satisfactory.

4.6.1 Thangka image retrieval based on the visual layer

Image retrieval based on the visual layer, that is, based on visual features of key region to make retrieval, its retrieval process show in Fig.14.

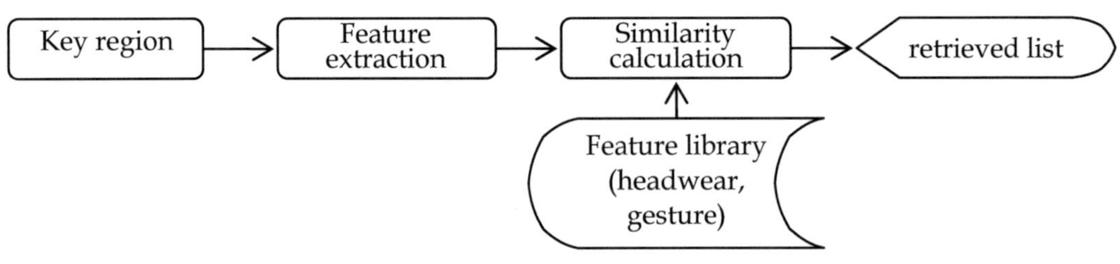

Fig. 14. Retrieval process of visual layer

Thangka image retrieval based on the headwear feature:

Headwear is an important characteristic in religion class portrait image, different headwear represent different category and have different meaning. First, the headwear's feature you specify image was extracted; then to calculate the similar distances between specify image and database images of the headwear feature one by one, ascending sort the similar distances; finally, to get retrieval image by some algorithm. There are 236 images in Thangka image database, the number are 53, 65, 118 for headwear as monk hat, bun, crown, respectively. Use 20 Thangka images as test sample, where 5, 5, 10 images have monk hat, bun, crown respectively. The precision and recall ratio for the top ten, the top thirty, the top sixty, the top one hundred to see Table 2.

		The top ten	The top thirty	The top sixty	The top one hundred
Monk hat	precision	78%	56.67%	39%	32%
	recall ratio	16.25%	35.42%	48.75%	67.08%
Bun	precision	82%	71.34%	59%	46%
	recall ratio	13.67%	35.66%	59%	76.33%
Crown	precision	88%	81%	73%	69%
	recall ratio	8.15%	22.66%	39.63%	63.52%
Average	precision	83%	69.67%	57%	49%
	recall ratio	12.69%	31.25%	49.13%	68.98%

Table 2. Retrieval performance of headwear

Thangka image retrieval based on the feature of gesture:

As with the process of Thangka image retrieval based on the headwear feature, precision and recall of the retrieval result based on the feature of gesture is 78.63% and 71.06%, respectively. Retrieval based on the feature of gesture with better retrieval performance compare with retrieval based on the headwear feature, duo to geometrical features of gesture are relatively easy to match, but the similarity of headwear feature are calculated by contour and color which appear contour similarity, similar color in many cases.

4.6.2 Thangka image retrieval based on the concept layer

Thangka image retrieval based on the concept of key region:

That is what is called Thangka image retrieval based on the concept of key region, first identifying key regions and extraction corresponding feature you specify, where key regions are the objects of this article mainly aim at the headwear and gesture, respectively. Different objects or regions have different feature, automatic annotation the concept of key regions you specify, and then obtain the final retrieval result with a concept. The flow shows in Fig.15 as fol1owing.

Experiment result and analysis:

The result of this experiment was: if the concept of key region was correct estimated you specify image, then all of images of inclusion the concept can be retrieval in image database, that is, recall and precision is 100%; retrieval result, instead, will be irrelevant with you

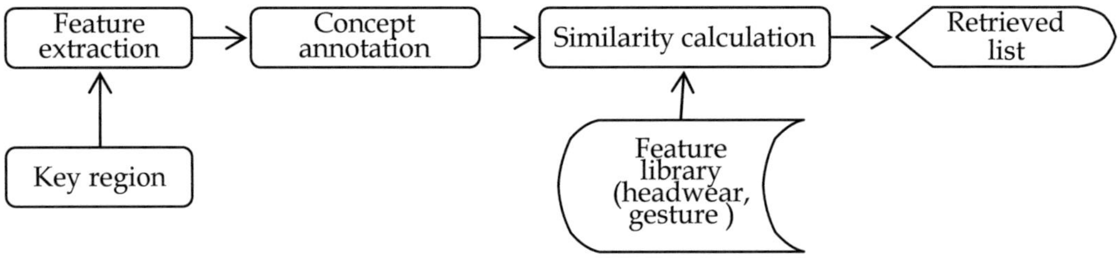

Fig. 15. Retrieval process of concept layer

specify image. In our experiment, there are 236 Thangka images in image database, test images 36, where 32 images' concept of key region was correct estimated, correct rate 88.89%. Therefore to improve the judging ability of key region's concept is very important, which need further study.

4.6.3 Thangka image retrieval based on C-K relation net

We employed 31 concepts, include 11 gesture and 20 musical instruments, 133 keywords. Each concept is described by several relevant keywords. First of all, annotate the interdependency of these 133 keywords by manual way, and construct *K-K* correlation matrix (keywords correlation matrix), where 0 indicates irrelevant and 1 indicates correlation. Because this part of experiment is pertain to natural language processing, thus, we apply manual annotation instead of analyze statistics of corpus. Second, six Thangka artists and six Tibetan teachers were invited to evaluate the membership degree that each keyword belongs to its relevant concept. The membership degrees were divided into three hierarchies, important, in general, and minor. The relevant weights of the three hierarchies are 1, 0.6, and 0.3 respectively. Applying Delphi method to appraise the evaluation and obtaining the final result of manual evaluation. And then, applying the degree of membership function this paper proposed to count the strength that every keyword belongs to other concepts based on *K-K* relation matrix. Composing manual evaluation and fuzzy statistics, we set the weight parameters ω_1 , ω_2 to 5 and 3. Thangka images are a description to religion culture. Thereby, their content of semantic object is standard preferably. The fuzzy statistics calculate the membership degree through counting the number of concepts which are described by semantic keywords. Based on the reason above, we give more weight to the part of manual evaluation. Finally, we obtain the retrieval result with CSM algorithm based on the *C-K* relation net, part of retrieval result as shown in Table 3.

In the semantic retrieval of natural image, the concept of normal semantic object is minimum granularity, whereas the minimum granularity of Thangka image is the semantic keywords which corresponding to semantic concept. And, the similarity between concepts depends on the interdependency of semantic keywords. Based on this attitude, we proposed a novel method apply on high-level semantic similarity retrieval of Thangka image. Firstly, construct *K-K* correlation matrix by manual annotation, and composing Delphi method and fuzzy statistics to built *C-K* relation net. Secondly, it is easy to accomplish similarity retrieval between concepts in the *C-K* relation net with CSM algorithm. Experiments indicated that the method can express the similarity relation between concepts accurately. However, this method only can satisfied similarity retrieval of concepts which inside the *C-K* relation net, and invalid for the retrieval of new concept.

Concept case	Retrieval result (top five)				
Tarjani-Mudra	Tarjani-Mudra	Hook-Mudra	Vajra-Vara	shield	Lotus
Anjali	Anjali	Lotus	Dhyana-Mudra	Humkara-Mudra	Dharmachakra-Mudra
Vajra-Vara	Vajra-Vara	Wisdom fist mudra	Eight-spoked dharma-cakra	Vajra bell	Trinacriform spear
Vajra bell	Vajra bell	Wisdom fist mudra	Rosary	Karma-vara	Lotus
Shield	Shield	Lotus	Sword	Humkara-Mudra	Hook-Mudra
Rosary	Rosary	Vajra bell	Shield	Spear	Lotus

Table 3. Part of retrieval result

5. Content-based Thangka image retrieval

The technology on content-based image retrieval (CBIR) is relatively mature, due to rich in color, picture complexity for Thangka image, however, some method for natural images are not always to suit Thangka image. A Thangka image retrieval system color-based and shape-based are intruduction.

Firstly, this part systematically studies extraction technology of visual characters about image's low-rise. On the basis of that, the typical extraction methods of characteristics of color and shape are respectively studied. Retrieval system for color-based and shape-based Thangka image are designed and realized. In addition, during the process of extracting color characters, an improved method called local accumulative histogram based on HSV is come up with combined with traditional local accumulative histogram and Thangka image's characteristics. Through many experiments, it shows that the color features seem to be more important than the shape features and the improved method called HSV-based local accumulative histogram is superior to traditional local accumulative histogram. Secondly, according to separate characteristics of color and shape, those two experimental retrieval systems are used to analyze the result Thangka image retrieval system. Then a comprehensive color-based and shape-based experimental retrieval system is designed and realized. After the experiment result analyzed, it is found that with comprehensive kinds of characteristics the efficiency of retrieving will be enhanced.

5.1 Retrieval framework content-based of Thangka image

A typical content-based Thangka image retrieval system as showing in Fig.16, which include two major contents[16]:

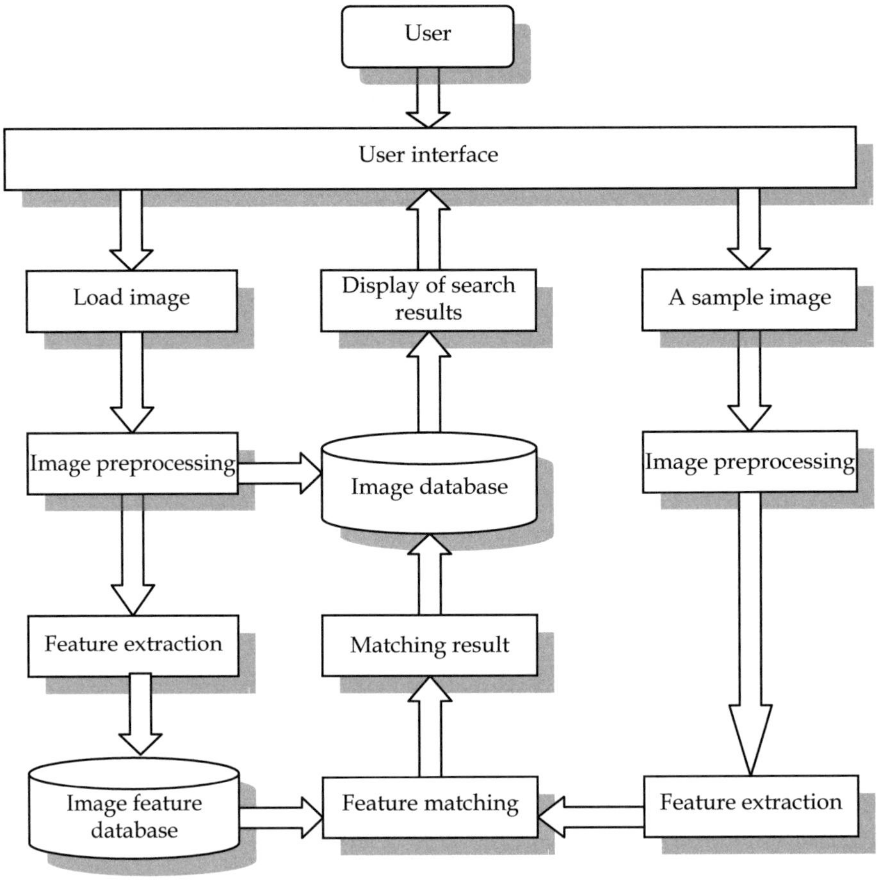

Fig. 16. Retrieval framework content-based of Thangka image

1. Establishment of Thangka image feature database. Left column from top to bottom, in Fig.16 establish the index mechanism between Thangka image database and Thangka image feature database.
2. Retrieving similar images. Right column from top, open a sample image or an image to be searched, the system obtain its feature by image preprocessing and feature extraction, then make similarity matching of feature between the specify image and database images, and the matching results are arranged in the order, in the top 20 search results will be feedback to the user.

5.2 Main contents

The key technology of content-based Thangka image retrieval is image feature extraction, this low-level vision features includes color, texture, shape and spatial relation etc. The retrieval methods for color-based and shape-based Thangka image are designed and realized. In addition, during the process of extracting color features, an improved method called local accumulative histogram based on HSV is come up with combined with traditional local accumulative histogram and Thangka image's characteristics. And a comprehensive color-based retrieval system and shape-based retrieval system are designed and realized.

5.3 Major results

1. The retrieval performance of feature color-based is superior to feature shape-based, and the retrieval performance of Color Moment-based is superior to other retrieval of color features.
2. An improved method of HSV-based local accumulative histogram which through to reasonably demarcate the HSV Color Space with second similarity measure is proposed, the retrieval efficiency are improved.
3. To achieve the color and shape of the multi-feature integrated search. Fig.17 is an interface of content-based Thangka image retrieval, to show the retrieval result by a sample image, and Fig.18 display top 20 similarity images.

6. Conclusion

The study aim of Thangka image's digital is cultural heritage protection, main content include inpainting of damaged Thangka image, construction of resource repository and information retrieval of Thangka. Although our research had made some progress in the domain, there are also many issues to be studied in further, such as image segmentation of damaged, inpainting methods, Thangka image annotation, how to obtain domain knowledge by automatic and semi-automatic way in order to reduce the manual involvement, and a practical system platform of integration inpainting, content-based and semantic -based Thangka image retrieval, which can efficiently realize all kinds of query in Thangka domain, will be further research contents.

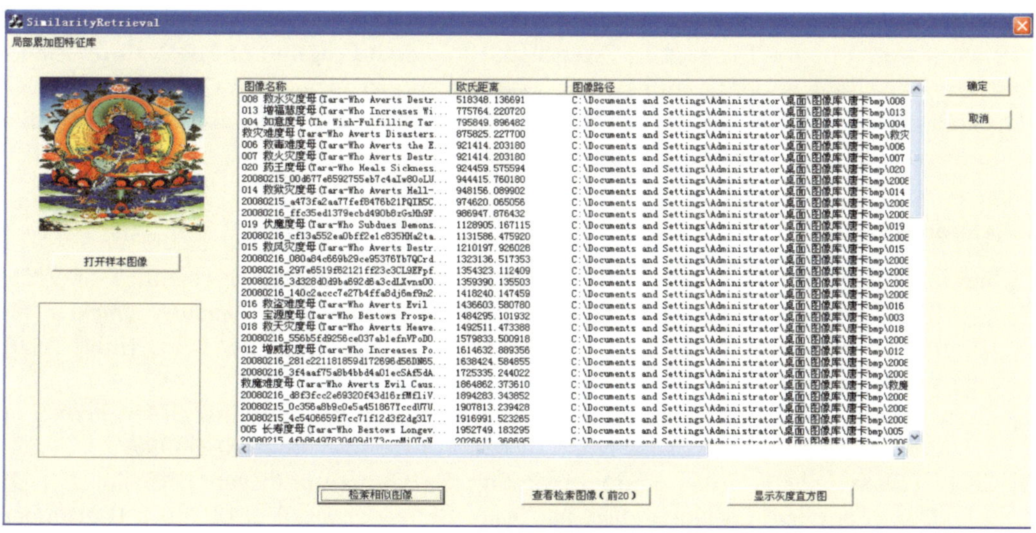

Fig. 17. Open sample image and similarity retrieval list

Fig. 18. Top 20 similarity retrieval list

7. Acknowledgment

This work was supported in part by Science and Research Program of The Nature Science Foundation of China under Grant No. 60875006, Gansu province under Grant No. 096RJZA 112, Science Foundation of Ministry of Culture〔2011〕820, and Innovative Team Subsidize of Northwest University for Nationalities.

8. References

[1] Bertalmio M,Sapiro G,Caselles V,et al.(2000).Image Inpainting.Proceedings of ACM SIGGRAPH, *Proceedings of the 27th annual conference on Computer graphics and interactive techniques,* ISBN 1-58113-208-5, New Orleans, LA, USA, (July, 2000), pp.417-424.
[2] Chan T,Shen J.Mathematical models for local non-texture inpainting. *SIAM Journal on Applied Mathematics,* Vol. 62, No. 3, (2002),pp.1019-1043, ISSN 0036-1399
[3] Chan T,Shen J.(2001).Non-Texture Inpainting By Curvature-driven Diffusions(CDD). *Journal of visual Communication and Image Representation,* Vol.12, No.4, (December, 2001), pp.436-449

[4] Bertalmio M,Bertozzi A,Sapiro G. (2001). Navier-stokes, fluid dynamics,and image and video inpainting, *Proceedings of the 2001 IEEE Computer Society Conference on Computer Vision and Pattern Recognition,* ISBN 0-7695-1272-0, Kauai, Hawaii, (December,2008) pp.355-362.

[5] Rane S,Sapiro G,Bertalmio M. (2003).Structure and texture filling-in of missing image blocks in wireless transmission and compression application, *IEEE Transactions on Image Processing.* Vol 12,No.3,(2003), pp.296-303

[6] Oliveira MM,Brian B,Ricard M et al. (2011).Fast digital image inpainting. *Proceedings of the International Conference on Visualization,Imaging and Image Processing,*Marbella, Spain, (2001), pp.261-266.

[7] Criminisi,Perez,Toyama. (2004). Region filling and object removal by exemplar-based image inpainting, *IEEE Transactions on Image Processing,* Vol.13, No.9, (September 2004). pp.1200-1212, ISSN 1057-7149

[8] Luc Vincent and Pierre Soille.(1991).Watersheds in Digital Spaces: An Efficient Algorithm Based on Immersion Simulations. *IEEE TRANSACTIONS ON PATTERN ANALYSIS AND MACHINE INTELLIGENCE,* Vol.13,No.6, (June 1991), pp.583-598, ISSN 0162-8828

[9] Wei Liyi,Levoy Marc.(2000). Fast texture synthesis using tree-structured vector quantization. *Proceedings of SIGGRAPH* 2000, ISBN 1-58113-308-1, (July 2000). pp.479-488.

[10] Bertalmio M,Vese L,Sapiro G and Osher S.(2003). Simultaneous Structure and Texture Image Inpainting.*Proceedings of the 2003 IEEE Computer Society Conference on Computer Vision and Pattern Recognition*, ISBN 0-7695-1900-8, Wisconsin,USA, June 2003. pp.1-6.

[11] Weilan Wang, Huaming Liu.(2009).Study of System Model of Image Inpainting Combining Subjective Estimation and Impersonal Estimation. *Proceedings of the International MultiConference of Engineers and Computer Scientists,* ISBN 978-988-17012-2-0, Hong Kong, March,2009, pp869-873

[12] Xiaobao Lu, Weilan Wang, Duojie Zhuoma.(2010). A Fast Image Inpainting Algorithm Based on TV Model. *Preceeding of the International MultiConference of Engineers and Computer Scientists. Vol II.* ISBN 978-988-18210-4-1, Hong Kong, March,2010, pp1457-1460

[13] Jianjun Qian,Wang Weilan.(2008). Main Feature Extraction and Expression for Religious Portrait Thangka Image. *Proceedings of the 9th International Conference for Young Computer Scientists,* ISBN 978-0-7695-3398-8, Zhang Jia Jie, Hunan, China,Nov.2008. pp803-807

[14] Jianjun Qian,Weilan Wang. (2009). Religious Portrait Thangka Image Retrieval Based on Gesture Feature. *Proceedings of 2009 Chinese conference on Pattern Recognition,* ISBN 978-1-4244-4199-0,Nanjing,China, Nov.2009. pp568-572

[15] Weilan Wang,Jianjun Qian,Lu Yin.(2010).High Level Semantic Retrieval of Thangka Image Based on C-K Relation Net. *Proceedings of the Fifth International Multi-Conference on Computing in the Global Information Technology,* ISBN 978-0-7695-4181-5, Valencia, Spain, September, September,2010. pp.77-81

[16] Xiaojie Li, Weilan Wang,Wei Yang.(2011). Content-Based Thangka image retrieval technology research. *Proceedings of 2010 International Conference on Image Analysis and Signal Processing,* ISBN 978-1-4244-5554-6, Xiamen, Fujian, China, April, 2011

Part 4

Distance Learning Through Multimedia

6

Multimedia Technology and Distance Learning Using Mobile Technology in Developing Countries

Sagarmay Deb
Central Queensland University, Sydney NSW, Australia

1. Introduction

The concepts of distance learning are prevalent in developing countries for last few decades and it is very much in vogue in developed countries [13], [17]. In the developing countries it started like many other countries did with correspondence courses where printed learning materials used to be despatched to the students at regular intervals and students were expected to read the materials and answer questions. The basic philosophy was teachers would be physically away from the students and have to conduct the teaching process from distance [15].

With the development of computer industry and internet networks during the last three decades things have changed and global communication has reached an unprecedented height [13]. With these developments immense scopes have come to the surface to impart learning in a much more efficient and interactive way. Multimedia technology and internet networks have changed the whole philosophy of learning and distance learning and provided us with the opportunity for close interaction between teachers and learners with improved standard of learning materials compared to what was existing only with the printed media. It has gone to such an extent to create a virtual class room where teachers and students are scattered all over the world. Although some of these facilities are expensive still the developed world is in a position to take advantage of these facilities to impart much better distance-learning to students residing in the developed countries. But for developing countries the story is different as computerization and network connections are still very limited compared to the developed world. In this chapter we focus our attention on defining the problems of using these technologies for much more improved and extensive distance-learning and suggest how we could possibly reach these vast majority of people from the developing countries with the improved quality of distance-learning provided by multimedia and internet networks.

Section one gives an introduction of the area. Section two presents the advancements developing countries are making to make use of mobile technologies. Section three presents the issue of usage of mobile technology with advanced multimedia tools in distance learning in developing countries. We put our concluding remarks in section four.

2. Analyses of works done

The open-universities which started functioning by late sixties and early seventies of last century, reaching off-campus students delivering instruction through radio, television, recorded audio-tapes and correspondence tutoring. Several universities particularly in developing countries still use educational radio as the main instructional delivery tool [13].

With the extended application of information technologies (IT), the conventional education system has crossed physical boundaries to reach the un-reached through a virtual education system. In the distant mode of education, students get the opportunity for education through self-learning methods with the use of technology-mediated techniques. Efforts are being made to promote distance education in the remotest regions of developing countries through institutional collaborations and adaptive use of collaborative learning systems [15].

Mobile learning refers to the use of mobile or wireless devices for the purpose of learning while on the move. Typical examples of the devices used for mobile learning include cell phones, smartphones, palmtops, and handheld computers; tablet PCs, laptops, and personal media players can also fall within this scope [8]. The first generation of truly portable information has been integrated with many functions in small, portable electronic devices [14]. Recent innovations in program applications and social software using Web 2.0 technologies (e.g., blogs, wikis, Twitter, YouTube) or social networking sites (such as Facebook and MySpace) have made mobile devices more dynamic and pervasive and also promise more educational potential [12].

Initially, computers with multimedia facilities can be delivered to regional resource centers and media rooms can be established in those centers to be used as multimedia labs. Running those labs would necessitate involvement of two or three IT personnel in each centre. To implement and ascertain the necessity, importance, effectiveness, demand and efficiency, an initial questionnaire can be developed. Distributing periodical surveys among the learners would reflect the effectiveness of the project for necessary fine-tuning. After complete installation and operation of a few pilot tests in specific regions, the whole country can be brought under a common network through these regional centers [15].

In developed economies, newer versions of technology are often used to upgrade older versions, but in developing economies where still older versions of technology are often prevalent (if they exist at all), the opportunities for leapfrogging over the successive generations of technology to the most recent version are that much greater [2].

In the conventional view, (i.e. as seen by technology developers and donors), developing countries passively adopt technology as standard products which have been developed in industrialized countries and which can be usefully employed immediately. However, successful use of IT requires much more than mere installation and application of systematized knowledge. It also requires the application of implied knowledge regarding the organization and management of the technology and its application to the contextual environment in which it is to be used. This implied IT knowledge often represents experience with the deployment of previous technology accumulated over time, such experiences contributing towards the shaping of new technology [2].

In addition to purely technological issues, the development of appropriate human resources skills are required, i.e. extensive training of the people who are going to use (and train others how to use) the resources. Training is seen as particularly important as this is not technology just a few people to benefit from, but for many. As Pekka Tarjanne, Secretary General of the ITU, made clear at Africa Telecom '98, "communication is a basic human right" (original emphasis). Nelson Mandela, at Telecom 95 in Geneva, urged regional co-operation in Africa, emphasizing the importance of a massive investment in education and skills transfer, thereby ensuring that developing countries also have the opportunity to participate in the information revolution and the "global communications marketplace"[2].

Canada's International Development Research Centre (IDRC) runs a number of developing country projects that involve technology leapfrogging. The Pan Asian Network (PAN) was set up to fund ICT infrastructure and research projects in developing countries across Asia. Individuals, development institutions, and other organizations should all be able to use the infrastructure so as to share information [2].

PAN works with Bangladesh's world famous grassroots Grameen Bank. One service here is a "telecottage", where network services can be obtained. The technology and the material will be tailored to meet the needs of Grameen's typically poorly educated clients. One of PAN's objectives is gender equity. Women, who constitute some 95% of Grameen's borrowers, will be prominent among PAN users in Bangladesh [2].

PAN is also responsible for linking Laos to the Internet. The Science, Technology and Environment Organization (STENO) of the Laos Government invited some Laotian IT professionals living and working overseas to return home and share their experiences with their colleagues in the country. STENO collaborated with PAN in designing an 18-month long project to build the necessary infrastructure for a dial-up e-mail service. Among the pioneer users were "researchers working on agriculture and aquaculture projects; journalists managing national news agencies and newspapers; lawyers consulting on international legal issues; travel agents planning business trips; computer resellers tracking down suppliers and obtaining pricing information; and about 20 others in both the public and private sectors" [11].

3. How to use mobile technology with advanced multimedia tools

In Section 2, we presented various efforts made to make distance learning effective in developing countries. Presentation of course materials through multimedia in remote locations where in villages there could be school structures where those presentations could be made is feasible. Of course learning materials must be self-explanatory and not boring. Using multimedia facilities like videos, audios, graphics and interesting textual descriptions, it is possible to reach the remote locations of the world where computer technology has not reached yet. As the areas not covered by computer and internet technology is still profoundly vast in the world this approach seems to be very constructive and should be pursued.

Wherever possible distance learning through multimedia should be imparted through internet as internet and networks are the vehicles of multimedia. But since bandwidth connection is still very limited in vast areas of Asia, Africa and Latin America it would still take long time to reach major part of the population of the above-mentioned regions with multimedia and web.

Mobile technology offers a very hopeful way to reach the vast population of the developing countries as it does not require bandwidth connections. We have to develop distance learning using multimedia through mobile technology. This seems to be the most viable way to reach billions living in the rural areas of the developing countries. Hence considerable research efforts must be dedicated to this line. Instructions could be sent through emails to mobiles of the distance learners. Also relevant website addresses could be transmitted to their emails and they could then visit those sites of distance learning though the internet of their mobiles.

In his book, Mayer (2001) declares that while learning from the text-only books results in the poorest retention and transfer performance, learning from books that include both text and illustrations and from computer-based environments that include on-screen text, illustrations, animations and narrations results in better performance [9].

Similar to e-Learning, mobile technologies can also be interfaced with many other media like audio, video, the Internet, and so forth. Mobile learning is more interactive, involves more contact, communication and collaboration with people [20].

The increasing and ubiquitous use of mobile phones provides a viable avenue for initiating contact and implementing interventions proactively. For instance, Short Message Service (SMS) is highly cost-effective and very reliable method of communication. It is less expensive to send an SMS than to mail a reminder through regular postal mail, or even follow-up via a telephone call. Further, no costly machines are required (which is clearly the case in terms of owning a personal computer).Besides SMS, distance learners can use mobile phones/ MP3 players to listen to their course lectures, and for storage and data transfer. New technologies especially mobile technologies are now challenging the traditional concept of Distance Education [21]. Today the more and more rapid development of the ICT contributes to the increasing abilities of the mobile devices (cell phones, smart phones, PDAs, laptops) and wireless communications, which are the main parts of the mobile learning. On the other hand for the implementation of mobile learning it is necessary to use a corresponding system for the management of such type of education [4].

The use of mobile technologies can help today's educators to embrace a truly learner-centred approach to learning. In various parts of the world mobile learning developments are taking place at three levels:

- The use of mobile devices in educational administration
- Development of a series of 5-6 screen mobile learning academic supports for students
- Development of a number of mobile learning course modules [5].

Research into the current state of play in Europe indicates:

1. There is a wide range of roles for mobile technologies supporting the learner in many ways ranging from relatively simple use of SMS texting to the more advanced use of smartphones for content delivery, project work, searching for information and assessment. Some proponents of mobile learning believe that it will only 'come of age' when whole courses can be studied, assessed and learners accredited through mobile devices.
2. Although books are now being downloaded onto mobile devices, the authors believe that to support the learning process a great deal of thought has to be given to the structure of the learning and assessment material. However, it is true that for some, mainly at higher education level, mobile phones offer the opportunity to access institutional learning management systems. This provides greater flexibility to the learner without any new pedagogical input.
3. Costs are coming down rapidly; new first generation simple mobile phones will not be available on the market from 2010. All mobile phone users in Europe will be using 3 or 4G phones within the next two years. A welcome associated step is a move towards some form of standardization by the mobile phone companies as exemplified by the shift to common charging devices over the next two years.
4. The value which is put on possession of a mobile phone, especially by young people is surprising and the data on ownership suggests that this will be a ubiquitous tool for all

very shortly and that it will be well cared for: there is evidence that ownership of devices brings responsible use and care.

5. Large scale educational usage in schools currently depends on government investment but in higher and further education it is safe to assume that all learners will have their own devices. Institutions will need to advise potential students on the range of devices most suitable for the curriculum, as they do currently with regard to computers. The convergence between small lap tops and handheld devices will continue until they are regarded as different varieties of the same species of technology.
6. There is a great potential for educational providers to work with large phone companies, both to reduce costs and to co-develop appropriate software [19].

Bangladesh Open University (BOU) is the only national institution in Bangladesh which is catering distance education in the country. It has extensive network through out the country to provide readily accessible contact points for its learners. After passing of 15 years since its inception, BOU has lagged behind in using technologies. In consideration of its limit to conventional method in teaching, a project was undertaken to test the effectiveness and viability of interactive television (TV) and mobile's Short Message Service (SMS) classroom and explore the use of available and appropriate technologies to provide ICT enabled distance tuition. In this project, the mobile technology's SMS along with perceived live telecast was used to create ideal classroom situation for distance learning through the Question Based Participation (QBP) technique. The existing videos of BOU TV programs were made interactive using this technologies and technique. The existing BOU TV program and interactive version of the same were showed to same learners of BOU to evaluate its effectiveness. It is found from the study that this interactive virtual classroom significantly perform well in teaching than BOU video programs (non-interactive) which is used at present [1].

Another paper presents and discusses NKI (Norwegian Knowledge Institute) Distance Education basic philosophies of distance teaching and learning and their consequences for development of a learning environment supporting mobile distance learners.

For NKI it has been a major challenge to design solutions for users of mobile technology who wish to study also when on the move. Thus, when students are mobile and wishing to study, the equipment and technologies they use will be in addition to the equipment used at home or at work. The solutions must be designed in ways to allow both users and non-users of mobile technology to participate in the same course. This means that we have looked for solutions that are optimal for distributing content and communication in courses, independent on whether the students and tutors apply mobile technology or standard PC and Internet connection for teaching or learning. The learning environment must efficiently cater for both situations and both types of students. The solutions were developed for PDAs. During the time of the development and research the technologies have developed rapidly. Mobile phones are including PDA functionalities and vice versa. In principle the aim of developments is to design solutions that can be used on any kind of mobile devices.

The paper builds on experiences from four European Union (EU) supported projects on mobile learning: From e-learning to m-learning (2000-2003), Mobile learning – the next generation of learning (2003-2005), Incorporating mobile learning into mainstream education (2005-2007) and the ongoing project, The role of mobile learning in European education (2006-2008).

Most NKI courses are not designed to function as online interactive e-learning programs, although some parts of the courses may imply such interaction with multi-media materials, tests and assignments. The courses normally involve intensive study, mainly of text based materials, solving problems, writing essays, submitting assignments and communicating with fellow students by e-mail or in the web based conferences. This means that most of the time the students will be offline when studying. From experience we also know that the students often download content for reading offline and often also print out content for reading on paper. All aspects and functions of mobile learning in the NKI large scale distance learning system is clearly an additional service to the students [3].

Mobile Assisted Language Learning (MALL) describes an approach to language learning that is assisted or enhanced through the use of a handheld mobile device. MALL is a subset of both Mobile Learning (m-learning) and Computer Assisted Language Learning (CALL). MALL has evolved to support students' language learning with the increased use of mobile technologies such as mobile phones (cellphones), MP3 and MP4 players, PDAs and devices such as the iPhone or iPAD. With MALL, students are able to access language learning materials and to communicate with their teachers and peers at any time anywhere [10].

4. Current limitations of mobile technology and how to overcome these

4.1 Current limitations of mobile technology

Every technology has some limitations and weaknesses, and mobile devices are no exception. They have shown some usability problems. Kukulska-Hulme summarized these problems as follows: 1) physical attributes of mobile devices, such as small screen size, heavy weight, inadequate memory, and short battery life; (2) content and software application limitations, including a lack of built-in functions, the difficulty of adding applications, challenges in learning how to work with a mobile device, and differences between applications and circumstances of use; (3) network speed and reliability; and (4) physical environment issues such as problems with using the device outdoors, excessive screen brightness, concerns about personal security, possible radiation exposure from devices using radio frequencies, the need for rain covers in rainy or humid conditions, and so on. It is important to consider these issues when using mobile devices and designing the learning environment [7]. We expect mobile producers would take care of these problems in the near future.

4.2 How to overcome these

However, looking at how rapidly new mobile products are improving, with advanced functions and numerous applications and accessories available these days, the technical limitations of mobile devices may be a temporary concern. Also, the use of mobile technologies in education is moving from small-scale and short-term trials or pilots into sustained and blended development projects [18].

The most serious issue faced by mobile learning is the lack of a solid theoretical framework which can guide effective instructional design and evaluate the quality of programs that rely significantly on mobile technologies. As Traxler pointed out, evaluation of mobile learning is problematic because of its "noise" characteristic with "personal, contextual, and situated" attributes (p. 10). Several attempts to conceptualize mobile learning have been made since the emergence of mobile and wireless technologies [18]. Traxler provided six categories by reviewing existing trials and pilot case studies in the public domain: 1) technology-driven mobile learning, 2) miniature but portable e-learning, 3) connected classroom learning, 4) informal, personalized, situated mobile learning, 5) mobile training/performance support, and 6) remote/rural/development mobile learning [18].

Koole developed a framework for the rational analysis of mobile education (FRAME) model which presents three aspects of mobile learning: the device, the learner, and the social environment. This model also highlights the intersections of each aspect (device usability, social technology, and interaction learning) and the primary intersection of the three aspects (mobile learning process) in a Venn diagram. What makes this FRAME model useful are the criteria and examples of each aspect and interaction and the checklist that might help educators plan and design mobile learning environments [6].

The definitions, technological attributes, and existing frameworks of mobile learning introduced above can help readers gain an understanding of mobile learning and how it is relevant to the future of teaching and learning with mobile technologies. However, previous studies and efforts suffer from the lack of a pedagogical framework. A number of the applications of mobile technologies in learning have shown a few links to established pedagogical theory. There is a need for the many different directions and unique applications to be logically categorized within the context of distance education. In order to better understand the current status of mobile learning and come up with comprehensive design guidelines for its future use, it is necessary to categorize educational applications with mobile technologies and position them in a logical framework. The transactional distance theory provides a useful framework based on sound theoretical and pedagogical foundations that can define the role of mobile learning in the context of distance education [12]. But as we know with multimedia technologies it's possible to combine more than one media like text, graphics, audios, and videos together in preparing study materials which go a long way in providing effective distance learning through mobile technologies.

5. Conclusion

In this chapter we studied the problems of imparting distance learning through multimedia in developing countries. We suggested mobile technology a viable and affordable media through which distance learning could be imparted to billions of people in an efficient way. We presented some examples of achievements in this field in this chapter where we can use telephone, photography, audio, video, internet, eBook, animations and so on in mobile and deliver effective distance education in developing countries. In the developed countries the majority of students already use their mobile devices to interact with and learn from the world around them and a world class room is created. They engage their current situation with texts, tweets, and Facebook updates to their friends. They yelp out for help finding a place to eat dinner and report back their findings. Some even use Goggles to find information about their surroundings from a picture. And they already do this in our class rooms [16]. But for developing countries it would take a while to reach this stage. More research needs to be carried out to tap the vast opportunity of reaching to billions in developing countries through mobile technology and gearing up multimedia technologies to be easily transported to those locations.

6. References

[1] Alam, M.S., and Islam, Y.M., "Virtual Interactive Classroom (VIC) using Mobile Technology at the Bangladesh Open University (BOU)", wikieducator.org/images/4/45/PID_563.pdf

[2] Davison, R., Vogel, D., Harris, R., and Jones, N., "Technology Leapfrogging in Developing Countries - An Inevitable Luxury?", Journal of Information Systems in Developing Countries (2000)

[3] Dye, A., and Rekkedal, T., "Enhancing the flexibility of distance education through mobile learning" The European Consortium for the learning Organisation, ECLO – 15th International conference, Budapest, May 15-16, 2008
[4] Georgieva, E (2006). A Comparison Analysis of Mobile Learning Systems. Paper presented at International Conference on Computer Systems and Technologies-CompSysTech' 2006. http://ecet.ecs.ru.acad.bg/cst06/Docs/cp/sIV/IV.17.pdf Retrieved on 31.3.2008
[5] Implications of Mobile Learning in Distance Education for Operational Activities, http://wikieducator.org/images/c/c6/PID_624.pdf
[6] Koole, M. L. (2009). A model for framing mobile learning. In M. Ally (Ed.), Mobile learning: Transforming the delivery of education and training (pp. 25-47). Edmonton, AB: AU Press, Athabasca University.
[7] Kukulska-Hulme, A. (2007). Mobile usability in educational context: What have we learnt? International Review of Research in Open and Distance Learning, 8(2), 1-16.
[8] Kukulska-Hulme, A., & Traxler, J. (2005). Mobile learning: A handbook for educators and trainers. London: Routledge
[9] Mayer, R. E. (2001). Multimedia learning. Cambridge: Cambridge University Press.
[10] "Mobile Assisted Language Learning", en.wikipedia.org/wiki/Mobile_Assisted
[11] Nhoybouakong, S., Ng, M.L.H. and Lafond, R, http://www.panasia.org.sg/hnews/la/la01i001.htm (1999)
[12] Park, Y. (2011). "A Pedagogical Framework for Mobile Learning: Categorizing Educational Applications of Mobile Technologies into Four Types", The International Review of Research in Open and Distance Learning, Vol 12, No 2, February 2011
[13] Passerint, K., and Granger, M.J., "A Developmental Model for Distance Learning Using the Internet, Computer & Education". 34, (1) (2000)
[14] Peters, K. (2007). m-Learning: Positioning educators for a mobile, connected future. International Journal Of Research in Open and Distance Learning, 8(2), 1-17
[15] Rahman, H., "Interactive Multimedia Technologies for Distance Education in Developing Countries - Introduction, Background, Main focus, Future trends, Conclusion", http://encyclopedia.jrank.org/articles/pages/6637/Interactive-Multimedia-Technologies-for-Distance-Education-in-Developing-Countries.html (2000)
[16] Rodrigo, R. "Mobile Teaching Versus Mobile Learning". EDUCAUSE Quarterly Magazine Vol.34, (2) (2011)
[17] Ruth, S., and Giri, J., "The Distance Learning Playing Field:Do We Need Different Hash Marks?", http://technologysource.org/article/distance_learning_playing_field/ (2001)
[18] Traxler, J. (2007). Defining, discussing, and evaluating mobile learning: The moving finger writes and having write... International Review of Research in Open and Distance Learning, 8(2), 1-12.
[19] "Using Mobile Technology for Learner Support in Open Schooling", www.col.org/sitecollectiondocuments/
[20] Vavoula, G. N. (2005). D4.4: A study of mobile learning practices. MOBIlearn project deliverable. The MOBIlearn project website. http://www.mobilearn.org/download/results/public_deliverables/MOBIlearn_D4.4_Final.pdf
[21] Yousuf, M (2006). Effectiveness of Mobile Learning in Distance Education, Turkish Online Journal of Distance Education-TOJDE October 2007 ISSN 1302-6488 Volume: 8 Number: 4 Article 9.http://www.google.co.in/search?hl=en&q =%22Effectiveness +of+Mobile+Learning+in+Distance+Education%22&meta= Retrieved on 31.3.2008